BATTLE L

TUNISIA, ITALY & PALESTINE
1943-46

GEORGE FORBES

Major the Reverend I.D.G.Forbes
OSB MBE MC TD CF

1st GUARDS BRIGADE

SAINT LAURENCE PAPERS XII
© AMPLEFORTH ABBEY TRUST

PAPER EDITION 2013
EAN/ISBN 978-0-9558357-2-8

This book is also available as a Kindle e-book
from Amazon (B00BHMHFFS)

Edited by Fr Anselm Cramer OSB
& Sue Goodwill
archive@ampleforth.org.uk

PRINTED BY AUTOPRINT, KEIGHLEY

NOTE ON PUBLICATION

Battle Diary, the account of his war experiences, was written by Fr George Forbes in 1947 or 1948 soon after his return to his Monastery. It was placed in the Archives of the Abbey and has been used by one or two researchers, but not otherwise published until now. One such researcher alerted us to the quality of Fr George's account, and on inspection this view seemed well-founded. It was first published as an e-book (for Kindle and its Apps), but it was quickly evident that those who had memories of this part of history were not naturally disposed to e-books & their devices (though we know one regular user of 96). Therefore we give here a paper version, especially for the market represented by the wider Ampleforth community, and for more senior military readers. We hope the world market (if there is one) will evade postage charges by opting for the electronic version. The differences are mostly of arrangement: the material is the same. Those who wish to make comparisons – favourable or unfavourable - are of course at liberty to purchase both editions. This will please the editor and publisher.

NOTE ON IMAGES

We have used such images as our archives could produce: some of them are elderly, or the originals were small, and without colour, as was then normal. Nobody had digital cameras or smart phones in those far-off days.

CONTENTS

APPENDIX

Second Lieutenant I.D.G.Forbes – Commissioned, Grenadier Guards, 1922

INTRODUCTION

IAN FORBES (he only became FR GEORGE as a monk, but used this name as a chaplain) was born in 1902 at Shrivenham (because his father was at the Staff College there), but the family home was in the eastern Highlands of Scotland, at Rothiemay. They could be called minor aristocracy: there is a photograph of Fr George's father leading the King and Royal family out at what looks like a Highland Games event, taken just after the war. Fr George was the eldest son. Four sisters outlived him, but not the youngest of the family, his brother Fr Charles (originally Drostan) Forbes, also a monk, who died in 1983. Fr George was at school at Ampleforth 1913-20, ended as Head of School, then passed 8th into the Royal Military College Sandhurst with a prize cadetship. In 1922 he passed out 9th and was commissioned into the Grenadier Guards.

However, the next year he resigned his commission and became a monk at Ampleforth. After ordination as a priest he taught mathematics, and in 1931 became C.O. of the College Cadet force (then the OTC). This gave him a lot of scope to train many of the young men who later became the junior officers of the armies which fought from Alamein to Lübeck. Not a few of them, like him, won the MC: he already had the MBE for his expert work on railway timetables for the schools joining the pre-war camps. He became a 'Chaplain to the Forces' (C.F.), as 'Captain the Reverend' in 1940, but did not leave England for three years. 'Major' came later. It was typical of him to evade the restrictions on the over-forties, and seize the first chance to move from 97 Field Hospital to the fighting troops in 1st Guard Brigade in Algeria.

They fought to Tunis, then were follow-up troops in Italy, where they plunged into the battles over the river Garigliano and on Monte Ornito. Here several MCs were won, the phrase *and maybe some more* being George's only reference to getting one himself. Conditions were awful. 'In really bad weather it took as long as thirteen hours to get a (wounded) case to a wheeled vehicle in this sector... It came on to rain at nightfall so heavily that we gave up any idea of sleep, and during the night it turned to sleet and hail with wind of gale force blowing.' This was without the efficient defensive activity of the German Army; and it should be added that much of the action in the next months took place on and among mountains up to 1000 metres high (3000 feet).

It was said of Fr George later, 'The strength of his character, which helped him to face calmly the horrors of war; sustained him in the uncertainties and cross-currents of the peace to which he returned.' To this he added a very real gift of compassion, and a lively sense of humour. In old age there was much to try him. He changed as little as he could while remaining loyal to the Church in its development. When I first knew him, he always said a Requiem Mass (for the dead, with black vestments, as was then usual) on any day it was allowed, and having read his account of the war, where death and burial were commonplace and often numerous, I can readily see why. On the other hand, he clearly liked, and was liked by, all, and found deep fulfilment in his pastoral care for the troops. Cheerfulness and happiness show all the time: even the brutal mountain weather of two consecutive winters did not wear him down. Not depressed by war or weather, he later found the changes of Vatican II incomprehensible, but was grateful to be allowed to stay with his Latin Breviary. It is remarkable that he was so often and so long under fire ('stonks'), yet untouched by wounds, even when a shell burst in the room he was in. As is often the case, he never spoke about his experiences: but his memoir tells a good deal between the lines. He seems to have written it straight through, relying on memory. A few small details, and perhaps some names (or their spelling), can be shown to be inexact in unimportant ways – 'south' for 'west', confirmed by the map – but it is clear that his memory was good and his account lively because free from pedantic concerns. It is for this reason that we have left explanation to the lists in the Appendix.

At the end of his life he was very deaf, no doubt from the years of battle. Nothing could be done for this: he must for a long time have suffered from the loneliness it brought; but, when one got through, his response was always amused, and amusing, with some story to tell. Fr George died peacefully, in the Infirmary of the monastery, on 4 July 1991, his legs still restlessly marching.

Fr George joined up as a Chaplain in 1940, but did not see action till 1943. He went originally with a hospital unit direct from camp at Westbury to Glasgow (Fr George at once detecting the details of the railway route), and then by ship direct to Algiers. This was part of the Anglo-American landing in French North Africa which balanced the Eighth Army advance from Libya, and resulted by May 1943 with the capture of Tunis, and the surrender of a quarter of a million German troops (probably as many as or more than they lost at Stalingrad).

Meanwhile Fr George had a stroke of luck when illness made a vacancy and he was posted as chaplain to the 1st Guards Brigade. After this Fr George, helped by the future Duke of Norfolk, Miles Fitzalan-Howard (or Howard), a former pupil, contrived to get involved in the landing in Sicily, including a visit to Malta. Then the Guards had to wait till after the Italian landings

(Salerno, Anzio) and went by ship to Naples. After that they were in the thick of the Italian campaign, including the battles round Monte Cassino, and were still hard at it around Venice when the Germans finally surrendered in May 1945. Fr George was further involved with the Guards, both in Austria and in Palestine, not returning to his monastery at Ampleforth till 1946.

He has added an Appendix dealing with the embarrassing part the Army was compelled to play in the return of prisoners into Soviet or Jugoslav hands, and with the difficulties which resumed after the war in Palestine before the end of the Mandate in 1948. All his accounts are written from the immediate perspective of a participant, who had no opportunity for hindsight, inside knowledge or awareness of any other point of view. Fr George was all the time in close touch with the men on the ground, and concerned principally for their well-being. Like many officers of the time they did not like what they saw, or suspected – it was indeed obvious enough at the scene of action – but they had been seeing many nastier things for several years, and were not asked for their judgement.

The document adds something to social history, for as an Army Chaplain Fr George had rank as an Officer, ending as a Major, and so lived and worked with officers, although he ministered pastorally to everyone, and included a good deal of practical as well as spiritual help for the wounded and the dead. Most of the people mentioned are names alone, except Colonels and Brigadiers (and above), when ranks are given. For the Army (and the social customs of seventy years ago) that is not surprising: it was then the same for everyone else. He evidently kept to their standards, for he could come out of the battle area and be greeted, 'Hullo, George! Dressed for Piccadilly as usual!' And he was 'thrilled to have spoken to both the Pope and the King within a month'.

The final judgement on Fr George's time as a Chaplain is not ours to make. But the award of the Military Cross, and his rather reticent way of referring to it – 'There were also several M.C.s given, [names], and may be some more.' – and the situations which brought it mark him out as an exception among exceptional men. Let his story speak for itself.

The Grenadier in 1922

9

The War in the South

In 1940 the Italians (Libya) attacked the British (Egypt) but were driven back. Hitler sent the German Afrika Korps (with General Rommel) to help, and he pushed deep into Egypt in 1942. At El Alamein General Montgomery (Eighth Army) won a set-piece battle with superior resources, and advanced steadily westwards to southern Tunisia. By then large British and American forces had landed at Algiers, but the Germans held them outside Tunis. It was at this point that Fr George and the 1st Guards Brigade became involved in March 1943 (First, later Fifth Army), and the Diary takes over. The later campaigns were the invasion of Sicily, then a two-pronged advance up Italy, much delayed by the tough (and skilful) German defence, with the US Fifth Army on the left and the Eighth Army on the right. They finished in Bavaria and Austria respectively. Subsequent work in Greece (to help the Greek government prevent a Communist takeover) and Palestine (to restrain a dangerous clash of interests), though important, were diversions.

The Guards

In Tunisia the units of 78 Division were re-organised as 6th Armoured Division, in which the 1st Guards Brigade were operated in principle as 'lorried infantry'. They were 3rd Battalion (Bn) Grenadiers, 2nd Bn Coldstream, 3rd Bn Welsh Guards. Often in the vicinity in were 1st Bn Irish and 1st Bn Scots Guards, who were part of 24 Brigade. This arrangement lasted till February 1945, when a new pattern was made with an eye on expected campaigns against mainland Japan, in the end not needed. Meanwhile (and elsewhere) other Guards battalions made up other Guards Brigades: some Guards spent all their time in England/Scotland (training) and in 'North-west Europe' (fighting, from 1944). Each battalion was made up of 3 or 4 companies, and the companies of platoons, but special groups drawn from Artillery, Engineers and Signals were attached either to a Division or to a Brigade, but could be switched about as need arose. Fr George, as a soldier twenty years before had been a Grenadier, but was officially attached for living purposes ('to the Mess') to the 2nd Coldstreams. As Chaplain he was appointed to the Brigade.

The Text

The text is pretty well as Fr George wrote it in 1947 or 1948, with very few corrections or breaks. We have added some commas, worked a few marginal notes into the main text, and divided one or two long sentences. There are 14 editorial notes, distinguished by [ ]. The Diary is written straight out, in three standard exercise books. No trace has been found of any previous sources, such as a log, diaries, letters or notes, but it would not have been unlike Fr George to have destroyed any such papers at some time since. But it reads as a fresh composition, not a laborious re-working. As he died in 1990 he cannot be asked.

Ampleforth

Ampleforth Abbey (1802) is a monastery of English Benedictine monks belonging to the English Benedictine Congregation (1218). It was first established as a community at Dieulouard in Lorraine in 1608, since monks were not at that time allowed in England. Its main work is running an independent secondary College (Years 9-13) of 600 students – the Abbey's Junior School is close by in Gilling Castle – but there is much work done in hospitality, and also in pastoral work in Benedictine parishes and in other ways. There are over seventy monks. For more see www.ampleforth.org.uk

Acknowledgments

We would like to thank the Abbot of Ampleforth for allowing the publication of Fr George's manuscript, Sue Goodwill for her transcription and copy-editing, Abbot Patrick Barry OSB for the material drawn from his Obituary of Fr George (*Ampleforth Journal* 96:2 (1991) 33), Lt Col. Conway Seymour of the Grenadier Guards archive at Wellington Barracks for checking some details, Lt-Col. John McKeown R.E. for guidance and advice, Fr Martin Haigh for the drawing of our church, and especially all those who have set up documents and articles on the Internet so that they can be shared.

CITATION
Rev (4th class) Ian George David Alastair Forbes

This officer was with my Battalion when occupying positions in contact with the enemy in the vicinity of Mt Ornito from 8 to 20 Feb. During this period the officer was constantly subjected to artillery, mortar and small arms fire and was attacked frequently. The conduct of this officer was beyond praise throughout. He showed a complete and utter disregard for his personal safety, and was always to be found where the battle was fiercest or the shelling most intense, giving courage to the wounded and dying, and inspiring the remainder by his contempt of danger. He frequently organised and accompanied parties to go forward from our position in order to bring in wounded. He was an inspiration to the whole Battalion, and I am not skilled enough with a pen adequately to describe his conduct.

Signed: **H.R. Norman**
        Lt Col commanding 2nd Bn Coldstream Guards.

Very strongly recommended. The same facts concerning this officer's conduct have been told to me by both the Welsh and Grenadier Guards as the results of his visits to them. He has indeed been an inspiration to all ranks.

Signed: **J.C. Haydon**
        Brigadier 1st Guards Brigade
Confirmed: **Lt-General R.L. McCreery**
        G.O.C.   X Corps

BATTLE DIARY

1 – TOO OLD AT FORTY
1 September 1942

TOO OLD AT FORTY must have come to most of us who have passed that age as a rather rude shock, and so indeed it did to me when it was announced that officers over that age would not be sent overseas. It was in October 1942, when events were moving towards the Anglo-American invasion of French North Africa, and I was already some months past that dreaded age. Up to then, from the time of my joining the army as a chaplain in September 1940, I had served with the 7th Guards Brigade in Somerset and Dorset for a year, in 3rd Infantry Division, living with the 33rd Field Regt RA commanded by Colonel Paddy Boylan, our role being one of defence on the South Coast against the threat of German invasion, until in September 1941 the Guards Armoured Division was formed. I was transferred to 6th Guards Armoured Brigade in that Division, then in process of assembling at Codford in the Wylye valley.

Brigadier Allan Adair asked me to live with the 2nd Battalion Welsh Guards in Codford St Mary [Warminster, Wilts], as they were without a chaplain. I had spent a happy year with them during the growing period of the Division, but, at the end of that time of experiment by trial and error, it was obvious that they would not be sufficiently trained for active service for at least another year. I therefore made up my mind to ask for a posting which would take me overseas, and on November 1st was duly posted to No 97 General Hospital.

I reported to Colonel Poston, the Commanding Officer, at Westbury and found that they were a newly-formed unit, complete as to male personnel, but without sisters, and waiting for their stores and all the other tedious processes that went on before a unit moved overseas. For a week or two I continued to look after my old Brigade till Father Ward relieved me. Then we had a fortnight's embarkation leave, and on our return settled down to wait for orders to embark, a wait which lasted all through December and January. Ordinary leave, in fact, reopened in January and it looked as if we were in for a long wait, which was all the more irksome as the North African landings had taken place in November and we heard of various other hospitals being sent out.

In the first week of February there were more definite signs. Our personal baggage was weighed and painted with cabalistic signs and numbers, none of which conveyed any meaning to us, and finally on February 20th 1943 we were confined to camp, and that evening entrained at Westbury station for an unknown port. My forty-first birthday had come and gone on the first of the month, but I was now an anonymous unit with only an army post official number for an address, and on the road at last.

The train left at 6 pm on a chilly and dark winter's evening, and it was possible to make out, in spite of the rigid black-out, that we had passed Reading and turned north through Oxford. There were only three in my compartment so we had a fairly comfortable night and next morning we were just north of Northallerton when our engine broke down, shedding its near-side connecting rod. While we waited for another engine I managed to say Mass in the guard's van, as it was Sunday, and had just finished when the new engine arrived. The journey continued uneventfully, broken by stops for hot tea at Newcastle and Edinburgh, and in the late afternoon we skirted Glasgow and reached our terminus at Gourock. Shortly after dusk we embarked by tender on S.S. *Circassis*, a 16,000 ton ship built for the Indian run and flagship of the Anchor Line, commanded by Commodore Bone. There were about 3000 troops on board of all kinds, including some Commandos who were on the lowest deck, well below the water line. In the officers' quarters we were not very crowded and I was lucky enough to be sharing a two-berth cabin with one of the ship's medical officers. The troop decks were, as always, very crowded and uncomfortable, but the meals were quite excellent, as is usual in a big liner, thought not of course quite as lavish as in peace time.

For the next three days we had leisure to settle down and to examine the ever-changing crowd of ships of all kinds anchored in the Firth. The Clyde was then, owing to the action of the Luftwaffe, the principal rendezvous of all shipping, whether inward bound from America, or outward bound for Egypt and India via the Cape, or Algiers by the newly re-opened Straits of Gibraltar, so the scene was always busy and full of interest. Final letters home were posted and we sailed at 10pm on February 24th.

2 – CONVOY TO NORTH AFRICA
February 1943

Next morning we had rounded the Mull of Kintyre and were heading west between Islay and the Ulster coast in rather rough weather. I had discovered that I was the only priest on board, and that there was a fully equipped altar in charge of a Catholic steward in the first class saloon, so I was able to say Mass, daily and twice on Sunday, during the voyage, except for the second day out when it was too rough.

There were twelve ships in the convoy, which included H.M.S. *Malaya*, with the usual naval escort of destroyers and sloops. For the next five days we made a big detour to avoid submarines and aeroplanes, going well out into the Atlantic before turning south east. The weather was good after the second day, getting warmer each day, till it was almost too hot to wear battledress. On the 2nd of March we were somewhere near the Canary Islands, and half of the convoy left us to continue their long trip round the Cape. We turned north east towards the Straits of Gibraltar, in company with the *Batory*, *New Holland*, *Boissevain*, the former a Polish liner and the two latter Dutch, and the Cunarders *Franconia* and *Letitia*, with our share of the naval escort vessels. We passed through the Straits of Gibraltar at midday on March 3rd, hugging the Moroccan coast and barely able to make out the Rock in the heat haze. Next morning we anchored at Oran at 8am and here we saw our first evidence of enemy action at sea, a larger tanker being towed in with her stern awash. We were anchored well off-shore and could not see much of the town. The *Franconia* and *Letitia* entered the docks and the rest of us sailed at dusk for Algiers. Next morning a Ju.88 appeared and our AA gun fired four rounds at it, whereupon it left us unmolested.

The approach to Algiers by sea from the west is dominated by the great basilica of Notre Dame d'Afrique, which stands on the headland to the west of the city. We reached the end of our pleasant voyage at midday on March 5th, docking in the harbour and disembarking by 3 p.m. on a very fine and warm day. The city of Algiers is built all along a steep hill rising directly from the waterfront, and we marched from the docks to a transit camp at Bouzarea, about 6 km away, a march which appeared to be uphill all the way. As our hospital orderlies were mostly category C men and were just out of the cramped quarters on the troopship, the marching was not very good and we had many very welcome halts.

The last of these was in the grounds of Benedictine nuns, and I was surprised to see a Benedictine monk approaching. He turned out to be the ex-Archabbot of Beuron (Abbot Raphael Walzer), who had fled from the Nazi regime, and was acting as chaplain to the convent. He was the first person that I spoke to in Africa, and was very kind and helpful during the next few days. The camp was a new one, just pitched on the top of a spur overlooking the city and adjoining the convent grounds, so I was able to use the chapel for daily Mass. The first night was comfortless as none of our kit had come up from the docks and we only had blankets and the bare ground to sleep on.

Next day we were reunited with our kit and could make ourselves fairly comfortable. Another General Hospital arrived, the Catholic chaplain being Fr Dowling, a Jesuit of the Irish province. On Sunday the 7th Fr Clarke, the S.C.F. of B.N.A.F., came up to see us, and told me that the chaplain with 1st Guards Brigade, Fr Bussy, had broken down, that he wanted me to go and take over the Brigade from him in Tunisia, and that I was to move as soon as the posting order came through, an enormous piece of luck, for it was the only Guards Brigade then in Tunisia and I hardly dared hope for a posting to it, though I did hope to get a fighting brigade somewhere.

There was a conference of Catholic chaplains in Algiers on the Monday, and there I met several of my colleagues and also Archbishop, now Cardinal, Spellman of New York, who had just been to Rome on a diplomatic mission to the Holy Father. He gave me a Greek corporal. I also met John Cowper in his office at A.F.H.Q. Next evening at dusk we had an air raid on the docks, just as 24th Guards Brigade were disembarking. It rained very hard and our camp became a quagmire.

Souk el Arba Station, Tunisia

On the 12th March I got orders to join a train, misnamed the Eastern Belle, which left shortly before midday for Souk-el-Arba in Tunisia, which was then railhead. I had a corner seat in an old second-class coach, full of officer reinforcements for the 36th (Irish) Brigade, mostly R. Ulster Rifles. Douglas Berry (Grenadier Guards) was also on the train. It took that train 24 hours to crawl up to Setif. I put down my valise on the floor for the night. We spent all Saturday and Sunday travelling through Algeria, with many stops to let westbound trains pass us, and reached Souk Ahras (Tagaste) on Sunday evening. Here they removed my coach from the train and I changed into an empty third class carriage, quite innocent of upholstery of any sort, and slept in it till the train restarted at daybreak. We crossed the frontier into Tunisia at Ghardimaou and got to the rail-head at Souk-el-Arba at 11 o'clock on the morning of the 15th.

The R.T.O. at Souk-el-Arba station directed me to a nearby transit camp, which like all transit camps seemed to have been dumped in a sea of mud in the middle of nowhere. I was only a few hours in it, however, and in the afternoon a T.C.V., taking reinforcements forward, transported me by way of Le Kef and Teboursouk to 'B' Echelon of the 2nd Coldstream in a farm

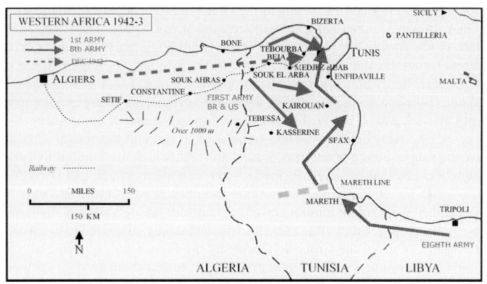

The campaign in Tunisia 1942-43

house near Testour. It was long after dark when I arrived, and John Baxendale, who had been injured in an accident and was back for a rest, got me a meal and shared his room with me. Next morning he sent me on by truck to Brigade, providing an air-sentry as well as a driver, for the main road to Medjez el Bab was then rather well known as a 'Stuka Alley'. We called at the Coldstream 'A' Echelon on the way, at a place called Sloughia, where Charles Harford was in command. Brigade Headquarters was in a large farm about two miles south of Medjez, and I reported to Brigadier Copland-Griffiths. Bill Pike was Brigade-Major and Dicky Paget-Cooke Staff Captain, but that day David Chetwode arrived to take over from Bill.

The Brigade was in process of being changed from 78th Division to 6th Armoured Division, and the Brigade staff was mainly 78th Divisional personnel. The 3rd Grenadiers and the 2nd Coldstream had been in the Brigade since the beginning of the war, but the 3rd Welsh Guards. Commanded by Colonel Edward Hodgson, had just arrived in place of the 2nd Hampshires (the Tebourba boys), and were in reserve with one company up, learning the ropes from the more experienced battalions. The Grenadiers were occupying Grenadier Hill to the east of the town, and the Coldstream were in the station area north of the town, facing Longstop Hill. The Mejerda river was the boundary between the battalions.

When it was dark Brigadier 'Cop' took me up to the Coldstream, to whom he had posted me, calling at the Grenadiers' headquarters on the way. There we saw Colonel Algy Heber-Percy and Victor Cubitt. The Coldstream R.A.P. was established in the railway station buildings, and there I met Elston Grey-Turner, the medical officer, for the first time, before going on to report to Colonel Bunty Stewart-Brown at the command post. I found Fr Gaffney, a White father who has since become the English Provincial, acting as a stop-gap till I arrived, and he went off next day to his hospital unit at Souk Ahras.

The rainy season still had some days to run and the forward troops were living in all the conditions of mud and filth which are familiar to those who knew the Ypres salient in the last war, conditions which had stabilised the battle for three months, ever since the unsuccessful dash for Tunis in December. The station buildings were at least dry, though slightly damaged by shell-fire. The stationmaster and his wife and family continued to live there. He had been given the Croix-de-Guerre by the French for collecting all the engines and rolling stock he could muster and sending them away to the west before the Germans could get them. After the battle he was promoted to be station-master of Tunis. He came and asked me to go to a farm and baptise a baby girl, Monique Bellier by name, as the church at Medjez was in ruins and the priest gone. This I duly did, receiving as a stole fee a present of a dozen eggs which was most acceptable.

I spent the next few days going round the battalions, making acquaintances and renewing old friendships, and also, at the request of Colonel 'Proggins' Price, went round the 102nd Field Regiment R.A. who were in support. I met John Cramer one day; he was a sapper in 46th Division and was up doing something with mines.

24th Guards Brigade had now arrived and had taken over on our left, so I went off to see Fr Rudesind Brookes who was with the 1st Irish Guards. That day I also saw Brigadier Dick Colvin, Jim Egan, and Tony Rochford who was killed a week later on Recce Ridge. On the 23rd the 1st Scots Guards (under Col John Dalrymple) took over the station area and we left at 2 a.m. on a hundred mile drive to the concentration area of 6th Armoured Division at Sakiet sidi Youssef on the Algerian border. We got in at 10 a.m. and were bivouacked in the pine woods, and spent most of the day making up arrears of sleep.

The next ten days were devoted to training and getting used to our new role of lorried infantry in an armoured division. I had a busy time going round the Catholics in the Brigade, and managed to see all of them. I also met Fr Dommersen, the senior Catholic chaplain in the division, and we were inspected by General Charles Keightley, the Divisional commander, who had been in No. 2 Company at Sandhurst in my time there.

3 – APPROACH TO TUNIS
April 1943

On April 4th, a Sunday as nearly always in the case of a move, we were moved to an area in the forest of Kesra, south of Maktar. The intention was for the Americans to break out into the Kairouan plain through the Fondouk gap, and for the armour to follow through to the sea at Sousse and cut off the retreat of the African Corps who were then being chased by the Eighth Army from their Mareth positions. The Americans unfortunately failed to make their breach in the line and this cost us 48 hours, till the Welsh Guards could mount a full scale attack on a vital feature. This they did brilliantly, but lost nine officers and a hundred men, including Dicky Twining who was killed while making his reconnaissance.

The job was well done, however, and the Armoured Brigade passed through the gap and took Kairouan. The infantry following up got dive-bombed several times by Stukas on the open roads in the plain and suffered some casualties. We were now in touch with the advancing Eighth Army who had taken Sousse, but the enemy whom we hoped to trap had slipped away to the north. The Eighth Army had enough troops to follow him up, so after a day's march northwards along an open road subject to frequent dive-bombing attacks, we were withdrawn by the way we had come to the forest of Kesra.

Just as we got back to our area at 5 a.m. the Coldstream had one of their many unlucky accidents with a T.C.V., which turned over, killing one of the men inside and injuring others.

Brigadier Cop left us at Kesra on appointment to the military mission in Washington, and Brigadier Stewart Forster took over command of the Brigade. After two days rest we were moved again by a long night march to an area north of El Aroussa.

Another attempt was to be made at a break-through to Tunis from the south by crossing the Goubellat Plain. Our area was very exposed and being without any shade was very hot by day. We were issued with khaki drill clothing and were very glad of it. Next day was Palm Sunday, and I was able to say three shortened masses with the blessing of the palms at each for the three battalions. There was much military activity in the area during the next three days. Gordon Watkins, who was Intelligence Officer with the Derbyshire Yeomanry, came to see me.

On April 21st we did another night move to near Goubellat and the battle opened at dawn on Maundy Thursday April 22nd with a barrage of 247 guns. We were stationary most of the day, and our R.A.P. dealt with a few casualties from 46 Division, who were doing the initial attack, mostly KOYLIs. The armour went in and we followed them, advancing very slowly for about 10 miles on Good Friday. There was a certain amount of hostile air activity and one of their planes was shot down by our A.A. Next day, April 24th, the armour got hung up in the foothills at a place called Sidi Nsib, north of the Sebkret el Kourzia and the Brigade debussed and pushed on to occupy the high ground north of the lake. We advanced about two miles into the hills and could look down on to the plain below where the armour was still trying to get forward without much success.

I went forward to visit No. 3 Company (Bob Windsor-Clive) and spent some time with Bobby Hyde in the forward area. A German gun was shelling the position spasmodically, traversing from the Grenadier position on the right, and we had one or two slight casualties. There was a good deal of air activity, nearly all German, and I watched them dive-bombing the armour for some time.

4 – EASTER SUNDAY IN FRONT OF TUNIS
25 April 1943

We were still fairly closely engaged next day, which was Easter Sunday, so only three people were able to get to my mass, which I said on the tail-board of my truck near the R.A.P. That night we were ordered to do an attack in an easterly direction on the flanks of a hill called Djebel bou Kournine which was strongly held by the enemy. The orders came late in the day, and the companies moved off at dusk. A thick mist had spread over the low ground, and we who were following up with the M.T. had a miserable night drive, lost our way and came round in a complete circle to where we had started from, and eventually came up with the battalion just before dawn. The attack had gone well – too well – and there were all the evidences of a hasty German withdrawal, including a Q.M. store full of new clothing.

Just as we were settling down and preparing breakfast the mist lifted and we saw where we were, cocked up on an open hillside within full view of the enemy on Djebel bou Kournine. It was not long before they opened up on us with all that they had, machine-guns, mortars and at least one 88 mm gun. Eighteen of our trucks went up in smoke in a few minutes, and the companies, which were only half dug-in, began to suffer casualties rather rapidly. The R.A.P. was, luckily, in a bit of a gully, so did not get a direct hit, and we soon had nearly 50 wounded, mostly walking cases. We had two ambulances from 1st Field Ambulance, so after nearly five hours of shelling and mortaring Elston Grey-Turner decided to load up the serious cases and try to pull out, as we could see that the companies were already withdrawing.

This we did with our five vehicles, and the Germans made no attempt to shoot us up, thanks to our Red Crosses. My driver, who had been lying very close like a wise man, drove out with the brakes full on till we smelled the burning brake linings. We made straight across country, through standing corn over which we could hardly see and which might have concealed all kinds of snags, to a rallying point down by the salt lake. Here the whole battalion congregated during the afternoon, except for No. 1 Company (Bill Harris) who were pinned down and could not get out till dark, together with Colonel Bunty [Stewart-Brown] who was with them when the shelling started.

We thought they would all be put in the bag, but they turned up all right during the night. No one had had any food for 24 hours, as the shelling started before we could get breakfast, in addition to our having been on the move all night. All the rations had been lost when the company trucks brewed up, so the R.A.P. turned to and made tea for the whole battalion. Never was a cup of tea more welcome. After tea Elston and I set off to go round the various dressing stations for news of our wounded. We found that they had been evacuated and that most of the A.D. stations were packed up and prepared to move. While we were at the Armoured Brigade A.D.S., just as dusk was falling, it was dive-bombed, but luckily the bombs missed by about fifty yards. So ended an exciting day.

The next day we spent in a harbour area by the salt lake, resting and re-organising, and watched with satisfaction the R.A.F. doing several bombing attacks on the Djebel bou Kournine. Our satisfaction would have been even greater if the attacks had come twenty four hours earlier, when the Germans were giving us such a bad time in what the men afterwards christened 'Blunder Valley'. Our casualties were 12 killed and 52 wounded.

It was evident that the armour could make no further progress in the hilly country east of the Goubellat Plain, so 1st Armoured Division remained on the ground in a holding role, and 6th Armoured Division was withdrawn into reserve in an area near Tallyho Corner. I took the opportunity of saying masses for the three battalions, and also of going to Thibar for some altar wine. The monastery of the White Fathers there is normally their novitiate, and is an oasis of peace and cultivation in the middle of a barren mountainous region, where their vineyards produce the best wine in North Africa. The monastery buildings were being used by a Casualty Clearing Station, holding all the lightly wounded, as the nearest General hospital was the at Guelma in Algeria and nearly a hundred miles away, and most of the serious cases used to go down to Algiers by hospital train, a distance of 500 miles.

What you see when a fuel or ammunition truck is hit

On Saturday, May 1st, we did a night move to a new area in the hills about eight miles south of Medjez. This was our final concentration area before the last battle of the campaign. There we remained for the next four days during which Colonel Bunty was called away to take command temporarily of 24th Guards Brigade who had suffered heavily in their battle on Djebel Bou Aoukaz. Colonel Roddy Hill came to command the 2nd Coldstream, and we were visited by Terence Falkiner who commanded the 3rd Battalion in 201 Guards Brigade. We found and buried some men of the East Surreys, an unpleasant task as the battle which they had fought on that ground must have taken place at least a fortnight before, and the African sun was by now getting rather hot. Elston and I took the opportunity of revisiting Medjez, where we found our old friend the station master in great form, and that the Germans had been pushed well back from Longstop Hill, so that it was possible to visit Chassart which had been battalion headquarters during the Longstop battles of Christmas Day.

The final battle for Tunis opened at 3 a.m. on Thursday, May 6th, with a barrage of 450 guns, the infantry assault being made on a two-divisional front on either side of the main road Medjez-el-Bab-Tunis. The 4th British Division was on the right and the 4th Indian Division, an Eighth Army formation which had been brought round from Enfidaville, on the left. They had close support from 500 aeroplanes in addition to the barrage, and this was too much for the German troops opposite them, so with little difficulty they were through to Messicault by the evening. Orders now came to the 7th Armoured Division

Tunis Station

23

(the Desert Rats) and the 6th Armoured Division to pass through the Infantry and drive straight for Tunis. We were on the right, behind 4th British Division and we were to have 201 Guards Brigade, which had suffered heavy casualties at Mareth, as right flank guard to watch for any threat from Djebel el Mengoub, which threatened our right flank. The 3rd Grenadiers were in the lead, so I attached myself temporarily to them, glad of an opportunity of going into action with the battalion that I had joined at Windsor in 1922 We began a long and slow move at 4 p.m. on May 6 which only ended near Massicault at dawn the next day. Opposition was not serious and we had little difficulty in crowning and clearing the hills that overlooked Tunis from the south. Meanwhile the armour pushed on and a race developed between the two divisions as to who should get into Tunis first. The two reconnaissance regiments got there almost simultaneously, but we of the 6th Armoured Division firmly believe that the Derbyshire Yeomanry beat the 11th Hussars by a short head – actually by a quarter of an hour in accordance with the wireless sitreps.

5 – AFRICA CLEARED
May 1943

As soon as Tunis had been entered the armoured divisions were ordered to turn outwards and drive the enemy along the coasts. It thus came about that 6th Armoured Division, being on the right, now began an operation which in the next three days administered the coup de grace to the Axis forces in North Africa. A long night move on the 7/8th and all the next day brought us to within sight of the sea east of Tunis and we could see the cathedral of Carthage across the bay to the north and the frowning mass of Djebel Bou Kournine overlooking Hammam Lif to the east. In preparation for forcing the passage of Hamman Lif, the Welsh Guards were put in to attack the high ground overlooking the town on the night of the 8th. This they did with conspicuous success and in the course of the action lost about 20 killed and 50 wounded. As they were rather thin on the ground, the 2nd Coldstream were put in at dawn on their left, so that on the morning of Sunday May 9th the heights above Hammam Lif were held by the Welsh & Coldstream Guards and all was ready for the attack by 26th Armoured Brigade with the 10th Bn Rifle Brigade and Grenadiers to follow up into the town.

This part of the country had been quite untouched by the war, and while we were moving into position for this vital battle the French were walking sedately to Mass in their Sunday best, called by the church bells, not two miles from a German 88 mm gun which was in action at the mouth of the defile leading to Hamman Lif and from which we suffered several casualties in the course of the morning. Casualties came trickling in from the battalion on the hill during the day, so in the afternoon I scaled the mountain and went round the companies, arriving in time to see the end of the armoured assault, when the Lothian and Border Horse stormed brilliantly along the beach and captured the town. I saw, too, the German 88 mm gun, knocked out by our Shermans and with its crew lying dead around it.

We followed the armour into the town and spent the night there, after some trouble with snipers. The town is a residential suburb of Tunis and the Bey's summer palace is there. The Bey himself, who had collaborated with the Germans, was caught trying to escape in disguise and a platoon of the Coldstream was detailed to take possession of the palace, from which the guard in its operatic uniform had fled, a job which entailed seizing the Bey's harem.

Hamman Lif sustained a good deal of damage from the tanks' guns. There was a big farm at the eastern end, and all the animals were gathered into the farmyard where a shell had killed the lot.

The next day the armour pushed right across the Cape Bon peninsula to the sea, thereby cutting off the German army from all their supplies and from any chance of escaping to Sicily. We followed up more slowly and bivouacked for the night at Grombalia about 12 miles south east of Hamman Lif. The 4th British Division which followed us forked left and over-ran the whole of Cape Bon. Many prisoners were coming in, mostly from base formations, who thought we were many miles away. We captured a field bakery in Grombalia, together with an indignant German baker who said he didn't want to be in any war but was quite happy baking bread in Bavaria. Also we found quantities of excellent Danish butter and cheese in tins, a very welcome addition to our ration margarine. All this was nothing to our experiences next day when we took up the pursuit to the coast. We travelled as fast as we could in a double column of vehicles, as there was no traffic in the opposite direction, and head to tail.

6 – A QUARTER MILLION PRISONERS
May 1943

It was a most inspiring sight to see the prisoners coming in by thousands to give themselves up. They were getting no supply of food or ammunition, so came in on foot or in their own vehicles looking for our prisoners' cages. The higher command had evidently not expected anything like the number that came in, 250,000 in all, and there was serious difficulty at first in coping with them. There was still a little sporadic opposition from individual Germans, but they soon saw the hopelessness of their position and gave in. No attempt was made to shell the ideal target which our column presented, and there was not one German aircraft in the sky.

We reached Bon Ficha airfield on the evening of the 11th and spent the night there. The fighting troops of the Afrika Korps were now completely surrounded in the hills, as our forward elements were only a mile from the Eighth Army at Enfidaville. All that night there was heavy gunfire. Either the enemy did not realise that he was trapped or he was getting rid of his remaining ammunition. At dawn on the 12th we moved again, this time in a westerly direction into the hills. We had just captured a German field hospital with staff and patients, including some wounded prisoners from the Eighth Army, when we heard that von Arnim and all his staff had surrendered to the 4th Indian Division, and the war in Africa was over. It only remained to collect the prisoners and the spoils, though there were isolated German units in the Djebel Zaghouan which held out for several days against the French.

In the German hospital we captured the only German chaplain I saw. He was Father Tomaschek, of Salzburg Diocese, and he told me he was the only Catholic chaplain with the 90th Light Division. On the 13th we had a Mass of Thanksgiving for the victory, at which Fr Tomaschek was present. That day we moved to the sea and encamped in an olive grove near Nabeul.

On the 14th I went into Tunis to look for Fr Rudesind at 24th Guards Brigade, and I found him at the 1st Irish Guards headquarters about five miles west of the city. He and I went back to Nabeul where we attended a dinner of all the officers of the three Guards Brigades. It was a most memorable occasion, and 191 officers of the 1st, 24th and 201st Guards Brigades were present.

We were not allowed to rest on our laurels for long. Barely a week after the end of the campaign, during which time I managed to get to Carthage and spend a night in the monastery of the White Fathers attached to the cathedral, we were moved away south to the area of Sousse. This town and port had been badly smashed by bombing and the harbour was blocked with wrecks which were being rapidly cleared in preparation for new ventures across the sea. We were camped outside the town in olive groves, the Grenadiers, with whom I was living for the time being, having their camp about three miles out to the south west near M'Saken. We had been temporarily loaned to the 1st Division in place of the 24th Guards Brigade, whose casualties in the Bon [area] had rendered them unfit for an active role pending the arrival of reinforcements.

The battalions took the opportunity of getting smartened up and also opened leave camps by the sea, and daily bathing became possible. The rainy season had almost spent itself, though we had one or two heavy rain storms. The weather was becoming quite hot, and the Grenadier Christmas Dinner, which was held on May 28th in a warehouse in Sousse, was hardly seasonable, but it was the first opportunity of having that feast that had presented itself.

7 – PREPARING TO CROSS THE SEA
June 1943

That Sousse was to be the jumping off place for a seaborne operation became obvious when the harbour filled with landing craft and the antiaircraft defences of the town were greatly strengthened. We had one or two air raids, but these did not disturb us unduly, though it is rather disconcerting to hear the whistle of fragments from our own shells descending when there is only a thickness of canvas between you and the sky. Our Brigade had been trained in amphibious operations in Scotland, so various boating parties to get used to the L.C.I.s were only in the nature of refresher courses.

On June 9th I rejoined the 2nd Coldstream and next day saw us marching down to Sousse and embarking on S.S. *Misoa*, one of the early experiments in landing ships. Evidently we were to be the 'follow-up' troops and were not

Landing beach, 'somewhere in Italy'

27

to be in the assault landing which was undertaken by the 2nd and 3rd Inf. Bdes in L.C.I.s, supported by a squadron of the Lothian & Border Horse in Sherman tanks. Our objective was now known to be Pantelleria, the 'Italian Malta', but when the convoy sailed at 4 p.m. we seemed to be going in the opposite direction, south east past Monastir, doubtless for the inspection of inquisitive hostile aircraft. Dawn found us off the island and we stood off during the morning watching the final bombing and bombardment by warships. The assault craft went into the little harbour at noon, and as soon as they touched down a forest of white flags went up over the whole island. The Lothians also went in and landed, though that was more in the nature of an experiment in landing heavy tanks than a necessity, as all opposition had ceased. Meanwhile information had come through that the island of Lampedusa had surrendered to a single R.A.F. aircraft, and one of the L.C.I.s came alongside to embark No. 1 Company under Bill Harris, to go and complete the occupation.

The Germans chose this moment to make an air counter-attack, and as we were the largest troopship there and were also stopped and unable to manoeuvre, we were singled out by two Focke-Wulfs for attack. The first dropped its bombs rather wide, but the second had two very near misses, one bomb dropping only just outside the port bow where I was standing talking to Peter Corbould, and another as near to the starboard quarter, the nearest misses that the ship had ever had. They did a certain amount of damage to the compasses, electric light and the landing ramp, but we had no casualties.

If the bombs had fallen inboard it would have been a shambles, as we were very crowded. There is no more helpless feeling than being dive-bombed in a ship, as you have nowhere to go for shelter. The Germans claimed to have sunk us. After this attack we went into harbour ourselves and touched down on the beach. Some administrative personnel were disembarked, but there was no need for us to do so. We got, however, our first close-up view of the effect of really heavy bombing, and it was terrible, hardly a house in the town being habitable. I saw a priest in a black cape starting to bury the dead, but of his church I could see no trace. At nightfall we returned to Sousse, arriving at 2 p.m. on the 13th, Whitsun-Eve, and there learnt that the other two battalions of the Brigade who were to have followed us had never even embarked.

During the month that followed we reverted to a non-operational role and prepared the camps through which the Eighth Army were to pass before embarking for the invasion of Sicily. These camps were named after football teams, that run by the Coldstream being called Blackpool, and we saw what an enormous amount of organisation was needed before launching an amphibious assault. The same thing was going on at Sfax and Tripoli, while the American expedition was mounted from Tunis and Bizerta, so what we saw was only a tiny fraction of the whole, mostly confined to a part of the 51st Highland Division, but it was none the less most impressive. There was, of course, much speculation as to the objective of the enterprise, and opinion was divided between Sicily, the heel of Italy and Greece, but security was good and no one on the lower levels seemed to know.

8 – FR GEORGE PLOTS A TRIP
July 1943

One day I saw Miles Howard by the road side. He was DAQMG of a 'Brick', or Beach Group, and had arrived in Africa about two months before. Between us we hatched a plot whereby I might be able to join the expedition, his share being that he would get me back to Africa when the assault landing was over. I then went to find
   Pat Tweedie, who was commanding a company in the Argyll & Sutherland Highlanders, and he took me along to Colonel Matheson, who made no

Probably officers of 2nd Bn Coldstream, summer 1943.
Fr George is sitting, 2nd from left

difficulty about taking an extra R.C. Chaplain as there was plenty of room in the H.Q. company's L.C.I. Then I had to obtain leave of absence from my own Brigadier and from Fr Clarke, as of course I was not being posted but was going unofficially, and also I arranged for my Brigade to be covered by a hospital chaplain while I was away.

All these arrangements having been satisfactorily made, I joined the 7th Argylls near M'Saken on Sunday afternoon, July 4th. We moved by M.T. in the evening to 'Brentford' area, which was being run by the Welsh Guards, and spent a short night sleeping on the ground, rather comfortless owing to the myriads of ants. We were, of course, on 'light scale', having with us only what we could carry.

Next morning we marched the nine miles into Sousse, which we reached about midday in the full blaze of the African sun, and we were very glad to embark on L.C.I. 183 and get out of our equipment. We sailed in a convoy of fifty-five at 2 p.m. and the ship's officers made us free of their very limited accommodation. It was one of the earlier landing craft, with tramway seats below decks and no bunks for troops, so we spent the night sitting up and getting what sleep we could in acute discomfort.

All we knew was that our destination was 'Finance', and it was only at dawn next morning that we discovered that 'Finance' was Malta. We entered the Grand Harbour, always a thrilling experience but doubly so on this occasion because we were the first troops to reach the island since the raising of the siege, and the harbour was full of wrecks sunk by the German aerial bombardment, including what was left of 'Ohio'. We disembarked on one of the hards at 6 p.m. and were taken to a camp up behind Hamrun where we remained till the 9th [July]. It was a heartening experience to see the warm welcome of the Maltese and their intense pride in being British, which even extended to the rule of the road, keeping to the left as in England and not to the right as we were so used to doing in Africa. We were living hard and sleeping on the ground in our camps, but apart from being assembled for an address by the Army Commander ('Monty' – in beret with two badges and pull-over as usual), our time was our own. I managed to do a bit of sight-seeing in spite of having no British money, which is the currency in Malta, and there was a Jesuit college just by our camp where I could say my daily Mass.

I rang up the Archbishop of Malta, but he was a sick man then and could not see me. We re-embarked in the same L.C.I. on Friday morning, July 9th. All the people in Malta said we were going to Sicily, but we did not know officially even then – all that Monty had said was that we were going to kill

Italians. Outside the Grand Harbour it was blowing hard, so much so that at one time it was almost decided to call it off, but the machine was too complicated to stop and we had to go on for better or worse. Never have I seen any craft that rolled like those L.C.I.s. Watching the rest of the convoy we could see their bilge-keels as they rolled over nearly on their beam-ends. I am not often sick at sea, but after the hot meals which was served between decks and was to be our last meal for an indefinite period, the sight and smell of everyone else being sick below were too much for me and I did not retain that meal for long. Luckily at sunset the wind dropped and the sea moderated, though there was still a heavy swell, which must have made the task of transferring the assault troops from the bigger ships to their small craft a nightmare. In fact Pat told me afterwards he thought they would never get it done.

9 – LANDING IN SICILY
July 1943

As we grew near to the shore in the dark it was a most comforting sight to see our bombing aircraft go over at almost mast-height to prepare the way for us. I suppose we were passing through minefields but nobody seemed to give them a thought. At last we had to go below and wait in our places for our turn to land. At 3.30 a.m. we grounded and the gangways were lowered. Quickly we passed down them in single file and followed the life line to the shore. It was a good landing, only waist deep if you kept to the line, and it was a surprise to find the water quite warm. The beach was not mined and the wire which was there had never been put up. Opposition was negligible and came from a kind of local militia. We had been told to expect up to sixty per cent casualties, but our battalion only had two killed and fourteen wounded, while I had two dead Italians to bury the next day and we took thirty-six prisoners. The rest of the opposition just melted away, and we strongly suspected that the swarms of men of military age who turned up next day in civilian clothes and smilingly offered to help us unload our stores were our late opponents.

Daylight was a welcome relief, as the warm sun soon dried our clothes and we were able to walk round the beach and take stock of our position. We had made our landing at Cape Passero, the extreme south-east tip of Sicily, and our battalion was the left flank of the Eighth Army. During the morning the Canadians began to land on our left. They had come straight from England, and looked pale compared to our men who had fought in the desert.

We did not move again that day, as we were waiting for our small quantity of M.T. to come ashore. It was most interesting to watch the scene on the beach, with all the tanks and guns and vehicles coming down the ramps of the landing craft and splashing through the water under their own power. Only a very few vehicles were 'drowned' and had to be winched ashore, which said much for the waterproofing which had been carried out in Africa.

After a very brief night we took the road at 2.45 a.m. and marched north past the town of Pachino, finishing at 7 p.m. near Rosolini. It was lucky that we had a long halt in the middle of the day, as the heat was almost unbearable. The vines gave us shade when we halted, and the grapes were just ripe and very welcome. All day we saw little sign of the enemy, our bag consisting of a few antiquated light tanks, possibly French. The Sicilians appeared either indifferent or friendly, and streams of them who had fled from the coast were returning to their homes, driving bullock-carts packed with household goods. As the Sicilian roads were mostly unmetalled, the dust and heat can be imagined.

When we halted for the night in the foothills we were bivouacked round a farm of some size, from which the occupants had fled. I was able to say Mass next morning in the deserted farm-house, and as there did not appear to be any prospect of an encounter with the enemy for some time (it was in fact nearly a week before they met the Germans hurrying from the west and fought the battle of Catania, in which Pat lost his right arm). I decided it would be as well to proceed with the second part of my programme and find Miles at his beach. I got a lift in a three-tonner to the coast and was lucky enough to fall in with one of Miles' officers, who took me to his headquarters. After lunch there I was advised to board a landing ship at Pachino port as soon as possible because it might sail for Malta at any time. I did so, and found L.S.T. 9 still discharging vehicles when I went on board at 6 p.m. This craft was a much bigger and better found ship than an L.C.I. and I was able to get a bunk in a cabin, as all the personnel were landing and she was going back light. My only companions were Julian Fane and Hugh Cumming with a small party of Phantoms, who had also found that their part in the assault had come to an abrupt end and were returning to Sousse.

We hauled off during the night, but did not sail for Malta as expected. Next day we went round to another beach further west and spent the day ferrying Canadians from the *Arundel Castle* to the beach near Porto Palo. At 1.30 a.m. on the 14th we sailed, and arrived off Malta at 8 a.m. and anchored outside. There was some doubt whether our ship was going on to Africa, and while they were making up their minds we saw the first British battle squadron to arrive at Malta since Italy entered the war sail in to the Grand Harbour. It consisted of *Nelson, Rodney*, the aircraft carrier *Invincible*, and attendant destroyers, a brave sight. At last orders came for us to transfer to *LST 320* which was going to Sousse, and we were ferried across in a small boat in a choppy sea, and had to climb up the side by a rope ladder, which we all achieved without mishap. Next day, July 15th, we arrived at Sousse at 2.30 p.m. and I was glad to ring up for my truck and get back to the Coldstream and out of my clothes for the first time for twelve days.

10 – AFRICA BECOMES A REAR AREA
August 1943

Thus ended my fighting experiences of 1943, for we spent the next seven months in Africa doing various non-operational jobs such as guarding prisoners of war and training. There did not seem to be much scope for an armoured division in the very close country where the Eighth Army and the Fifth American Army were fighting, and many people thought that we would either be sent home to take part in the invasion of France or that we should remain in Africa for the rest of the war.

We remained at Sousse till the beginning of August and then the Brigade was moved from Tunisia to Algeria, the Coldstream going to a camp on the sand dunes just east of Bone, the Grenadiers to Guelma with detachments at Souk Ahras (Tagaste), the Welsh Guards to Constantine and Brigade headquarters to La Calle, very widely dispersed. About this time Brigadier Philip Gregson-Ellis arrived to take over from Brigadier Stewart Forster. I spent the rest of the month doing a tour round the various detachments and interviewing the men. The chief points of interest about the neighbourhood were that Bone was the ancient Hippo, the see of St Augustine, and Souk Ahras was Tagaste, his birthplace. I was at Hippo on August 28th and said Mass in the Basilica there, afterwards assisting at High Mass of the feast sung by the Archbishop of Carthage, Primate of Africa, a White father, and at the subsequent lunch I met him and the Bishop of Constantine and Bone. At Bugeaud on the mountain behind Bone there was a unit of Phantoms and I saw Hugh Fraser and Johnny Macdonald there.

On September 9th the Brigade concentrated at Constantine, Brigade Headquarters and the Grenadiers in the town and the Coldstream and Welsh Guards in a forest about five miles outside. This forest was a splendid place for a summer camp, as it was delightfully cool, but in winter it was still a quagmire and very cold, being a thousand feet up or more. The rest of 6th

Armoured Division was concentrated at Robertville between Constantine and Philippeville, and we were free of such duties as guarding prisoners of war, and engaged in training for future operations. We were not to be used again till the following February, and then piecemeal, one Brigade at a time, so we missed the Salerno landings and all the operations in southern Italy, nor were we chosen for the Anzio landing in January 1944. It was pleasant to be at peace again for a spell, and to see the city of Constantine ablaze with lights, after our four years of black-outs.

On October 5th Colonel Hugh Norman arrived to take over command of the 2nd Coldstream from Colonel Bunty Stewart-Brown who had led the battalion since the landings at Algiers in November 1942, had been wounded and awarded the D.S.O. at Longstop, and who now left for England, to our great regret, and was later killed in France with the 5th Battalion, a great man and a most gallant leader

11 – JAUNDICE
October 1943

About this time we had an epidemic of jaundice (infective hepatitis) among the officers of the Brigade and many were to be found in No. 31 General Hospital, which was established in a French T.B. hospital at Oued Athmenia, some miles west of Constantine, an elevated and chilly locality, as those who had the misfortune to be in the overflow tents outside the buildings found to their cost.

I succumbed to the epidemic on October 25th, getting the disease rather badly and spending the next four weeks in that hospital, at first in the building but later in a tent. It was an unpleasant experience, tempered by the excellent care of the hospital staff, and by the presence of many friends, either as fellow sufferers or visitors. We also received a fair number of casualties from the fighting in Italy, most of whom had been flown back to Africa, among them being Michael Reyntiens who had lost an eye serving with the 2nd Scots Guards.

On my discharge from hospital on November 21st I returned to the Brigade, but was still feeling very weak and ill, so did not feel up to facing the life in the forest, sleeping in my truck and slopping about in the wet. I accordingly went to live with the 3rd Grenadiers, who were partly in billets and partly in huts on the outskirts of Constantine. I found myself a billet in the diocesan Seminary, which was only a hundred yards from the Grenadier officers' mess, and I was given a comfortable bedroom there. It was a joy to have a proper bed with sheets after sleeping for so long in a flea-bag on a camp bed, and the only disadvantage, the fact that they locked up at 9 p.m., did not worry me much, as I was glad enough to get to bed early.

A month passed, during which my strength gradually returned, and when Christmas approached I returned to the Coldstream in the wood, as the Grenadiers were entertaining the 16/5th Lancers for the Christmas period and their mess was very full. I found that more than half the battalion was away at Tunis, guarding the Prime Minister during one of his meetings with President Roosevelt [*vere* staying with Gen. Eisenhower, returning from Tehran Conference], a commitment which lasted some weeks, as Mr Churchill fell ill with pneumonia. The remainder of the battalion was under the command of Bob Coates, recently arrived from England, and the Welsh Guards, under Colonel Willie Makins, who had succeeded Col Edward Hodgson, were in the adjoining camp. It was a very cold and wet Christmas and snow fell early in the New Year, so I returned to my billet in Constantine on January 2nd, as I was still rather unfit.

12 – SAILING TO ITALY
February 1944

The first month of 1944 passed in much the same manner, the only variation being the move of battalions in turn to a training area among the sand dunes and cork forests east of Philippeville. Colonel John Prescott came out to visit the Grenadiers, and Charlie Huntington left to command the 5th Battalion, with which he was killed at Anzio very shortly afterwards. Brigadier Philip Gregson-Ellis also left the Brigade about this time, to assume command of 5th Division in Italy, and his successor, Charles Haydon, came out from England to Italy direct and met us there when we landed.

We left Constantine on February 3rd and drove down to the docks at Philippeville and all three battalions with Brigade Headquarters and 1st Field Ambulance embarked on S.S. *Ville d'Oran*, a 10,000 ton C.G.T. ship which in peace time plied between Marseilles and Algiers. We could only take assault scale equipment with us and no transport, as the latter was to be shipped separately from Bizerta, so that was the last I saw of my truck for three weeks. I took with me my bedding-roll, less camp bed, and portable altar, in addition to the usual equipment, and was therefore able to exist in some sort of comfort. I was still attached to the Grenadier battalion, and Ewart Williams, their M.O., and I shared a two-berth cabin which seemed to be very full of his medical panniers and had no port-hole.

We sailed at 7 a.m. on the 4th and made a very rapid passage by ourselves with two sloops as escort. All that day we skirted the North African coast, identifying such places as Bone, Carthage and Pantelleria. During the night we passed through the straits of Messina, and barely 24 hours after leaving Phlippeville we were sailing past Capri into the Bay of Naples. It was a great thrill to return to the continent of Europe, and to make that particular landfall, and I think most of us were glad to be out of Africa at last. A bitterly cold wind greeted us from the north as we sailed into the Bay, bringing a foretaste of what we were to endure during the next two winters in sunny Italy.

Naples, as seen from the sea on February 5th 1944, was rather disappointing. The water front has been entirely ruined by factories, and these had been heavily bombed and looked the picture of desolation. The docks were full of damaged ships, and had not been operating very long, while the chief impression of the remainder of the city during the short drive by jeep to the railway station was one of sordid squalor, dirt and poverty. The bleak wind brought a further promise of grim times ahead.

We entrained at what was left of the main station of Naples in two trains of box wagons and eventually set off on a wearisome journey to Capua, which took some seven hours though the distance is only twenty one miles. From Capua we were moved in 3-tonners by a General Transport Company R.A.S.C. to a small town called Cascano, and finally got into our billets at 3 a.m. on Sunday morning. I toured the town at about 9 o'clock and found a notice on the parish church door to the effect that there would be Mass for troops at 10 o'clock, so I waited till then and Fr McCabe C.P., Senior Catholic Chaplain 10th Corps arrived. I said the Mass while he heard confessions and preached. I then discovered that only the Grenadiers were in Cascano, the Coldstream being in Sessa Aurunca, a Cathedral town nearby, and the Welsh Guards at Teano.

13 – RIVER GARIGLIANO
February-March 1944

But we were not left in our billets for long, as the situation was rather critical at that time. A bridgehead had been forced over the River Garigliano by Commandos (under Sir Walter Cowan) and was being held by the 46th Division, which had fought all the way from Salerno and was a very tired formation. We were to move over the river and take over the centre of the bridgehead on a brigade front and eventually to continue the advance and capture Monte Maio, the biggest mountain in that area, an ambitious programme which might have been possible for a Corps but was hardly on for a Brigade. On Monday afternoon [7 Feb.] we moved off in M.T. and were debussed (before dark) on the forward slope of the valley near Roccamonfina.

There followed a long march in the dark, down to the Garigliano, along its banks and over 'Skipton Bridge', then over a range of foothills to a maintenance area named 'Harrogate' and on to the foot of Monte Juga, which we reached just before dawn. We spent the day resting there and the next night we started to climb the mountains. There were no roads in this region and all supplies had to be moved by means of mules and porters. These mule tracks were quickly churned into mud by the unusual amount of traffic, so all walking in the mountains of Italy was a real feat of endurance, and the evacuation of casualties by stretcher was a nightmare. The stretcher cases had to be carried every yard of the way by bearer-parties in relays every few hundred yards and in really bad weather it took as long as thirteen hours to get a case to a wheeled vehicle in this sector. The bearers, mostly Indians, were marvellously patient and careful in doing what must have been a heartbreaking task.

It poured with rain during the Tuesday night and I woke up to find the hole I had made for my hip full of water and my blankets wringing wet. I thought it must be near dawn and looked at my watch, to find it was only 9 p.m. The rest of the night was sheer misery. Next day I discovered that the Grenadiers were in the reserve position and were practically not engaged, and that the Coldstream were holding the left half of the sector on Monte Ornito while the Welsh Guards had the right half on Monte Cerasola. The orders to both battalions had been to take over the ground from whoever was occupying it, British or German, and a good deal of it being German-occupied, vigorous action was required before we were satisfied with our positions.

The situation was, to say the least, uncomfortable. The Welsh Guards were just short of a razor-backed ridge which ran the whole length of their position and bent back at right angles on the right flank. The Germans were just the other side of the ridge, not fifty yards separating the forward posts, and both sides kept up a game of shuttlecock with grenades and mortar bombs. The Coldstream held the top of Monte Ornito, the highest point, Point 759, being held by Ian Skimming's Company (No. 2), and an underfeature, Point 711, about three hundred yards further forward and sticking out right in front of the general line, being held by Henry Green with No. 3 Company. For the next ten days the Germans did everything in their power to push us back across the Garigliano, counter-attacking one or other of the positions every twenty-four hours, and though they succeeded at times in getting a footing in our line they

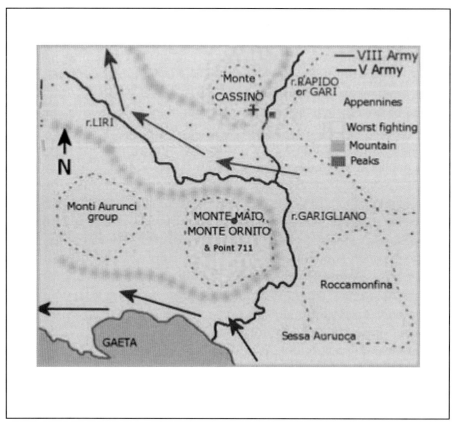

Monte.Cassino and Monte.Ornito &.Maio: Allied advance, Jan-May 1944

were always flung out again, and, when we were eventually relieved, we were able to hand over the line intact, and the Germans had given it up by then as a bad job.

As the main stream of casualties was coming from the other two battalions I left the Grenadiers and moved to the Coldstream R.A.P. This was in a sangar on the reverse slope of Monte Ornito, with the Welsh Guards R.A.P. in a kind of sheepfold about two hundred yards further down the hill. It was an unpleasant spot, as all the German shells which missed the top of the hill came sweeping down the mountain-side, following the contour of the ground, and one always had an unpleasant feeling that if one stood on tiptoe the shell might crack one's head like the top of a boiled egg. There was also the chance of a shell getting tired and falling in our midst, which did happen now and then, though most of them went on to burst harmlessly on the rocks below. The whole area was also within range of the German mortars and we had quite a number of casualties from them as well.

The first night in that position was one of the most unpleasant I have ever spent. It came on to rain at nightfall so heavily that we gave up any idea of sleep, and during the night it turned to sleet and hail with a wind of gale force blowing. To crown it all the Germans opened up with their mortars at five a.m. as a prelude to one of their frequent dawn attacks. Luckily next day was dry and sunny and we were able to get our clothes dried.

During the morning I walked over to the reserve company (No. 1). Tom Jackson was sitting outside his headquarters with Peter Crowder, and he stood up to greet me. A lump of metal fell just where he had been sitting, and he remarked: 'This seems to be my lucky day'. Poor Tom – that afternoon No. 1 Company were ordered to dislodge some Germans who had established themselves near Point 759, and he was hit in the head as he led the company forward, 'Get on, never mind me,' he said to his Company Sergeant Major, and the attack went in successfully. When they returned they found Tom had been hit by one of our own shells and killed. We had already lost Michael Hilton-Green killed in that place, and also Arthur Farnell-Watson, the Pioneer officer, who had been wounded in the leg by a piece of one of our own shells which fell short. The Gunners O.P. also received a direct hit from a mortar which killed or wounded everyone inside, the Major having both his legs blown off.

On Saturday the 12th I went round the forward companies, which entailed some very rough walking over boulder-strewn slopes, up over the col to the west of Ornito and down the other side, then up to the right again to Point 759, and down and up again to Point 711. It was interesting, because one could see the twin villages of Castelforte and Santi Cosmo e Damiano, which were German-held, and the rough open ground that lay between us and them, pitted with shell-holes. It was necessary, too, to move with caution, as there were snipers within range who could cover part of the ground. The forward companies were very exposed and it was quite impossible to dig in that ground. By degrees they built up sangars with the boulders, but it was slow and heavy work. While I was there some casualties had to be evacuated and I tried to help, but found it very difficult, hard enough to keep one's own footing without dealing also with a fourth share of a stretcher. I pitied the unfortunate wounded. Theirs was inevitably a rough journey.

14 – A CASUALTY PROBLEM
12 February 1944

We had rather an unfortunate contretemps in this sector over casualties. Both sides had been collecting wounded under the Red Cross flag, and some stupid Guardsman opened up with a Bren gun near one of the German stretcher parties. They retaliated by shooting up our stretcher-bearers and hit Gdsn Thorogood, one of my Catholics, rather badly in the arm and leg, to his intense indignation. It was a pity that this misunderstanding arose, as it made the problem of collecting the wounded much more difficult. On the whole both sides respected the Red Cross and it paid to do so.

Another curious incident of the same kind occurred on Cerasola. A German stretcher party wandered over to our side of the ridge and were promptly made prisoner. This led to a parley under the white flag between a German officer and David Gibson-Watt, in which it was arranged to return the Germans in a week's time through another part of the line. When the week was up they begged to be allowed to remain as prisoners.

On Sunday the Brigadier, Charles Haydon, came round. I had met him for a moment in the dark during the march up to the line and of course I knew him by reputation. I was much struck by his asking for H.C. and kneeling out to receive it on the hillside in front of everyone. He was a grand leader and the Brigade would do anything for him, and he was the only Brigadier who

Monte Cassino: the Monastery seen high above the town about 1930
This was the Guards' position in 1944

acquired from us a 'pet name' – we called him Uncle Charles. Afterwards I went round the battalion and gave H.C. to Ben Faller, Reggie Secondé and some others, as there was no chance of saying Mass at all during this time.

By now we had got ourselves much more organised and Elston [Grey-Turner] and I were sharing a sort of scrape in the ground covered by a bivouac tent where there was just room for both of us to lie down together. Battalion Headquarters was just above us up the hill and No. 3 Coy under Henry Green with Michael Hollings next to them in reserve. They had been relieved on Point 711 by No. 4 under Bob Palmer. No 1 was also in reserve, having suffered heavy casualties in the attack when Tom Jackson was killed. The next four days passed in much the same way, with frequent attacks and raids by the Germans, and each day I managed to get to one or other of the forward companies or to the Welsh Guards on Cerasola. I had a lot of burials to do of all denominations, as both the other Brigade chaplains were sick, and some of these graves were on the forward slope facing Castelforte as it was not easy to get the bodies back any further. It was not a good place for a cemetery, as the ground was liable to be shelled, and I fear some of the graves were obliterated later.

On Thursday the 17th Bill Birkbeck and Roddy Sheridan were brought in in the early morning with big holes in the back of the leg. We also heard that Ben Faller had been badly hit on Point 711, so Elston and I went forward to him. He had a nasty chest wound and was very distressed so I anointed him, and this calmed him down a lot, in fact I was told that he soon insisted in getting off the stretcher and walking down the hill. The Germans had gained a foothold in No. 4 Company's area, and while I was there a counter-attack was put in to drive them out, led by Stephen Whitwell. It was very successful, as a stream of Germans came running over the crest with their hands up, including one officer. It helps morale a lot to see the other side give in like this.

We were then told that there were two or three of Ben Faller's platoon lying out in front wounded. Owing to the misunderstanding about the use of the Red Cross Bob Palmer decided to send out some men under cover of smoke to search the ground. Corporal Pickford, the stretcher-bearer corporal of No. 4 was in charge and about twelve of us went, co-opting a German stretcher bearer from among our prisoners. He was a plucky little man and very willing to go. The Germans reacted rather strongly to the smoke and turned on a couple of Spandaus, so we experienced the not very pleasant sound of bullets whistling through the air, rather like the rustling of silk. Only one man was hit, however, in the jaw, and as we found no wounded but only dead bodies we returned rather quickly when the smoke began to blow away. Whether we would have achieved more by trying a Red Cross flag and trusting to luck is an open question, as we were acting on information given by our prisoners and that may have been a ruse to get us out into the open. In the eventual check-up I think we accounted for everyone. On February 15th we could see the bombing of the Monastery at Monte Cassino, about 12 miles away to the north, through our field glasses.

15 – MONTE ORNITO & POINT 711
16 February 1944

The next day saw a renewal of the attack on Point 711 with more casualties to evacuate and more prisoners, a total of fifty prisoners in two days, and on Saturday the 19th the Germans made a really determined attempt to drive a wedge between the Coldstream and the Welsh Guards at dawn. It was a very nasty moment when we realised that they had actually got a footing on the hill above Battalion Headquarters, but the subsequent counter attacks restored the situation and resulted in another hundred prisoners. It was carried out by the reserve companies and a company of the Hampshire Regiment, the company commander of which was rather badly wounded in the arm by a stick grenade. Elston was out at the time so I took him to the stretcher post of 1st Field Ambulance which was at the foot of a gully that we called Hell Fire Corner. They had been having a bad time from mortars during the attack and had lost two of the R.A.M.C. men killed and three wounded, so were just packing up to move elsewhere, but 'Queenie' Gordon, the M.O. in charge, opened up again to deal with my wounded officer and carried on quietly and competently till he was bandaged up, despite a fair plastering

Leaflet 'fired over our lines'. But Tower Bridge is shown still standing.

of mortar bombs. They continued to mortar us all day, largely out of spite, I suppose, on account of the failure of their big attack.

A Grenadier company had relieved No. 4 on Point 711, much overdue as they were for relief, but it was quite impossible to carry it out while they were under incessant attack. The whole area had livened up and there was fairly continuous shelling. I went up to Point 711 with Eric Stern and we found that Peter Maclean, the Company Commander, had been killed by a stray shell. I gave H.C. to Corporal Byrne and another man, and found the company not at all happy about the situation, though Tony Denny who was now in command seemed to take it calmly enough. The Brigade were to be relieved that night, so I spent the day helping to tidy up the battle area by getting all the rest of the dead that we could recover buried.

I walked down the hill in the afternoon, a long and weary tramp, to Brigade Headquarters at a small village called Suio on the Garigliano. During the fortnight's battle, which will always live in the memories of those Coldstreamers and Welsh Guardsmen who took part, we had held the line intact and inflicted heavy loss on the enemy. Brigadier 'Joe' Kendrew, who commanded our relieving brigade and who liked to see things for himself, went out in front of Point 711 by night and said that he had never seen so many German dead in any one place before.

I was glad to get down to Brigade, where Tom Faber had found a spare camp bed for me, and I had a really good meal. All the staff were out seeing to the relief, except Geoffrey Howland-Jackson, the staff captain, who embroiled me in a religious argument that lasted till midnight.

16 – SUPPLY DIFFICULTIES
February-March 1944

One of the biggest difficulties of the Ornito battle was the absence of roads. All supplies came down a Jeep track by Jeep train through Lauro and over Skipton Bridge, the track being so narrow that it would only take one way traffic, so that all traffic was suspended while the Jeep trains were on the road. The track was also under observation and shell fire from Minturno. Once across the river the supplies were transhipped to mules, which carried them up the hills, a distance of may be seven miles as the mule walked, to an advanced dump called 'Cheshire'. This camp was an unpleasant spot, as the enemy had spotted it from the air and used to shell it at regular intervals, usually at fixed times. From there all supplies were carried forward by porters, mostly Basutos and Indians, who worked extremely well in spite of several casualties. Bob Coates, the 2nd in command, worked the supply problems, as he spoke Hindustani. His daily arrival at battalion Headquarters was most welcome, and he brought us lots of much needed kit, leather jerkins, gloves, new socks and so on.

From the medical point of view the chief difficulties were the long carry in evacuating casualties, and the cold and wet which resulted in cases of frost-bite and trench foot, and which caused our water-bottles to freeze at night. I can recall Gdsn Farrer spreading out Elston's blankets to dry in the sun one afternoon and leaving them too late, so that they froze solid, like enormous water biscuits. In compensation we had a marvellous view, when we had time to look at it, over the sea in the Gulf of Gaeta and to Vesuvius in the distance with its red lava stream (it was in eruption at the time) glowing in the dark.

Colonel Hugh Norman had led the battalion magnificently throughout the action, and got a well-earned immediate award of the D.S.O. There were also several M.C.s given, including Bob Palmer, Stephen Whitwell, Elston, 'Doris' Davies-Scourfield, Dai Gibson-Watt (a bar), and may be some more. [The closest Fr George came to mention his own award.]

After a good night's rest I returned to the other side of the river, up the Lauro track, and through Sessa to a small village called Casale where the Coldstream were billeted. I was suffering much from sore feet and Gippy tummy, so was glad of the rest. While at rest we were addressed by General 'Ginger' Hawkesworth, commanding 46th Division, who had several complimentary things to say. We were under command of 46th Division at this time and in Xth Corps which was then commanded by General McCreery.

I found an AA Brigade H.Q. in Casale with Fr 'Natty' Ord as chaplain, so we worked the area between us as my Brigade was rather scattered, and in that way we got a lot of Easter duties done. On Monday the 28th of February I went in my truck, which had by now rejoined us, to Naples and saw Ben Faller in No. 92 General Hospital. Fr Angold of Buckfast was the chaplain to that hospital and I also ran into Fr Vincent Cavanagh, who had just done a tour of duty in the Anzio beach-head.

On my return I discovered that the Welsh Guards and Grenadiers were to go into the line again, but on the right of the 4th Divisional troops that had relieved us. The Grenadiers were to take over Cerasola this time, with the Welsh Guards on their right on Monte Purgatorio, a much smaller hill which filled the gap between Cerasola and the Garigliano. The position faced due north and was overlooked by the Germans, which made movement by day rather restricted. I arranged to join Dai Morris in the Welsh Guards R.A.P., and moved forward independently, spending a night at the A.D.S. of No. 1 Field Ambulance at Skipton Bridge, where Colonel Sandy Sangster was in charge. This was a farm tucked well under the hill, and the German shells all went over to burst on the other bank of the river.

Our two bridges, Skipton and Pateley, were pontoon road bridges, and gave constant anxiety to the Sappers, as the Germans controlled the sluices and used to release the water every now and then in the hopes of washing them away. Just by Skipton Bridge there was a hot sulphur spring, and the Sappers had made a bathing pool out of it, no doubt very healthful, but the smell of bad eggs put me off. The whole area had been heavily mined by the Germans, particularly in the orange groves, where the fruit was now fully ripe. One small but enterprising boy had watched the Germans doing this mining, and though he would not part with the information he used to go into the groves himself and bring out the fruit, which he sold for large sums to the soldiers. On March 2nd I went to the forward A.D.S. which was at Harrogate, the mule base, and said Mass for them there, then went on to join the Welsh Guards. The R.A.P. was in a dilapidated bell tent on the hillside, and as they had not really room for me there I went back about a mile to a farm house which was their supply point. Here I shared a room with the four Welsh Guards officers who were running the supplies, Elladwr Williams, Charles Brodie-Knight, Willie Bell and John Egerton. It was interesting to see the difference of organisation of this battalion from the Coldstream. They had four officers where we normally had one, or at the most two, and relied more on the C.Q.M. Sergeants to get the supplies forward to their own companies.

17 – FISHING FOR INFORMATION
March 1944

It was a comparatively quiet area, except for shelling, mostly 'overs' from Ornito. I spent most of the next seven days walking up to the battalion and going round the companies. On one occasion I found Colonel Algy (Heber-Percy) up on the crest of Cerasola fishing for a German body with an enormous 'fishing-rod' made for him by John Cramer, one of the 46th Division Sappers. It was a large pole with a pulley on the end over which passed a rope with a grapnel attached, and he would make a 'cast' over the crest, then have about five Guardsmen tailing onto the rope to drag in whatever the grapnel caught. He got two or three dead bodies that way, but I don't think they were much use for identification purposes as they had been out for some time. Colonel

Algy was full of terrific energy as usual, and as the Germans were not troubling him much, he expanded his energies on improving the position, rebuilding the sangars, making a road along the whole of his front which he christened 'Ye olde Grenadier Way', and collecting something like two hundred man-loads of salvage. I returned to the Coldstream at Sessa on the 9th, as the newly-arrived S.C.F., Fr Bright (now [1947] Auxiliary Bishop of Birmingham), wanted a conference. This was held at 10th Corps Headquarters near Cascano, and on the next day I went to see John Magrath at Francolise, where he was I.O. to 23rd Armoured Brigade Headquarters.

The following day was a Sunday so I went back in the afternoon to the other side of the river, calling at the Franciscan monastery at Roccamonfima, and spent the night at Brigade H.Q. returning to the Welsh Guards on Purgatorio next morning. I went up to Ornito one day to check over the graves there, and met Grant, the C. of S. Chaplain with the 6th Black Watch, who used to be minister of Rhynie, and then went to Cheshire where I found Fr McHugh, whom I had relieved at 7 Guards Bde in 1940, in the A.D.S. There it rained most days and snowed on the high ground at night. During this period there was a great bombardment going on at Cassino both from the air and the ground. The Coldstream relieved the Welsh Guards on the 15th and I was able to move forward again to the R.A.P. as Elston had room for me there. We were living entirely on compo rations during this time, everything being brought up by mules, belonging to an Indian unit, as there were no roads at all in the area which would take wheeled traffic. We had some leaflets fired over us by the Germans about the V1 raids on London, very poor stuff which only made us laugh. [*Vere* July 1944]

18 – VESUVIUS
March 1944

On Sunday 19th I went back to Brigade as we were to be relieved next day. I was lucky this time in getting a mule to carry my kit to 'Palm Beach' supply point whence I got a Jeep along the riverside road to Brigade, which saved a very long walk. Our new billets were in a small and very dirty town called Sorbello. On the 24th I took a day off and went in my truck to Sorrento to see the Irish Guards who had just come out of the Anzio beach-head. We went through Naples and along the road between the sea and Vesuvius, then in full eruption. The shower of ashes was so thick that we had to put on our headlights. All the women were out in the streets weeping and praying for the wind to change, which it did later on, carrying the ashes over somebody else,

Monte Cassino Abbey: reconstruction 1955

but the men were all on the flat roofs, shovelling off the ash for all they were worth lest the accumulated weight should break down the houses. One could picture just how Pompeii was overwhelmed. The lovely Sorrento peninsula was rather spoiled by this coating of grey ash which covered everything, though very good for the crops I was told.

I found the Micks at the very end of the road in a place called S. Agata. They had suffered very severe casualties in Anzio, and shortly afterwards they returned home. I saw Colonel Andrew Scott and Fr Rudesind, but could not stay long as I had to get back to Sorbello that night.

After a quiet week and we were moved to a little village at the foot of the Matese Mountains, called San Potito Sannitico, where the whole Brigade were together, mostly under canvas. This was to be our base for some weeks and it was very pleasant there in the early Italian spring, except for some winds of gale force which blew the tents down. We kept our reinforcements and 'B' Echelons here all during the Cassino battle and it was always a pleasant place to return to for a few days' rest, as the war had passed quickly by and there was very little damage. The rest of 6th Armoured Division was gradually concentrating in the Piedemonte-Alife area, so we were all getting together again at last.

We were not left long in peace, as on the 30th the Grenadiers were put in the line again, this time on the Cassino front just to the left of the New Zealand Division's sector south of Monte Trocchio. It was a thrill to drive up Route 6 through Vairano and Mignano and under the shadow of Monte Cassino where 201 Guards Bde had fought their famous battles at Christmas time. We there diverged onto the 'speedway', really the track of the Naples - Rome railway from which the rails had been removed to make a maintenance road. I

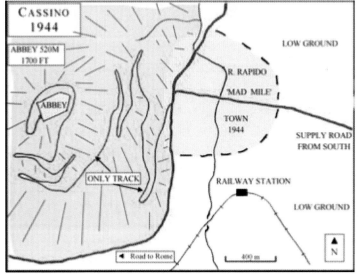

Cassino, town and hill, fought over for six months

off-loaded at the R.A.P. and sent my truck back to San Potito, which was just as well, for it would certainly have been hit if I had kept it. The R.A.P. was in an outbuilding of a farm, the farm-house being occupied by the reserve company. This building got two direct hits in the night, killing a sergeant and giving John Penn a very narrow escape. Colonel Algy had got jaundice, so Pat Needham was commanding the battalion. It was supposed to be a quiet area, nevertheless there was a good deal of shelling which went on for long periods, but we did not stay very long, as our next job was to be in the town of Cassino itself.

19 – CASSINO TOWN
April 1944

I returned to the Coldstream on April 3rd, attending on the way an Eighth Army chaplains' conference at Piedemonte d'Alife where I met also Bishop Gawlina, the Polish senior chaplain. I found that, owing to our heavy losses at Ornito, No. 1 Company had been placed in suspended animation, and a company of Scots Guards had come to the battalion. This was known as 'S' Company and it remained with us for nearly a year, covering itself with glory in that time. It was commanded then by David Cuthbert with Andrew Neilson as second in command. Eddie Trafford was one of the subalterns and most of the men were young soldiers fresh from England. We held a battalion parade on the 4th which I watched with Gordon Watkins, our divisional press officer, who used to be I.O. of the Derby Yeomanry in Africa. It was a great contrast next day to move from the peace of San Potito to the hell of Cassino.

On the 5th of April, it being the Wednesday in Holy Week, the battalion left to take over the centre section of the town from the New Zealanders. We had a longish drive, first over the bad roads round Alife and across a long Bailey bridge over the River Volturno, then up the great highway Route 6, on both sides of which every possible camping place was occupied by some unit. We halted near Mignano for an evening meal, and then began the forward move which was to become so familiar, the cross-roads with the military policeman which had an evil reputation for being shelled, Monte Porchio, then Monte Trocchio behind which the guns roared continuously and round that final bend at Pastinelle where one came into full view of the monastery. Beyond that point it was impossible, turn which way you would, to avoid the menace of that sinister hill.

By now it was dusk and we turned off the main road down a lane which led to S. Pasquale and Brigade Headquarters. Another lane led us to the debussing point, close to a cemetery which had been heavily shelled and stank to heaven. There we loaded ourselves up, those who were staying in the town with all their kit, and sandbags wrapped round their boots, the porters who were coming out again weighed down under their Everest packs. From there we walked in single file and in dead silence, up to the main road again at Two Corpse Corner, whence it led straight as a die for half a mile to the main German defence position. It was here that the 'Mad Mile' really began. A hundred yards further on two Bailey bridges side by side spanned the Rapido river, one or other of which was sure to be out of action through shelling, maybe both. On this occasion the right-hand or upstream bridge was all right, but the crossing on the wooden floor sounded terribly noisy.

During all this time our guns were firing smoke shells to hide our movement from the monastery. We subsequently asked the Germans what they made of this, and they said it suited them well, as they did their supplies at the same time and our smoke screen did for both. Up the steep ramp to the road again, and then onto a different world. The bombardment of the town had entailed the dropping of 1100 tons of bombs within a square mile and the devastation had to be seen to be believed. The trees alongside the road had all been shattered and on either side enormous bomb-craters lay full of water. Every building had been razed except a solitary telephone kiosk. Naturally every yard of the road was registered by the German gunners and in addition there were two Spandaus, one of which fired from the Hotel Continental straight down the road, the bullets keeping rather to the southern side and rather high (we always walked on the right or northern side!), and the other which used to come out from somewhere in the station area and fire across the road, unpleasantly low. Spandau Joe and Spandau Willie we called the two gunners, and a very uncomfortable feeling they always gave us.

Half way from the bridge to the town we passed a knocked-out tank with a scissors bridge, which had tried to reach and bridge the father and mother of all bomb craters right in the middle of the road. Skirting round this formidable hazard we came to the real foetid stench which overhung the whole of the town, the smell of dead bodies which it was impossible to bury. There was the body of an American nurse there: she had come up from Naples to see the sights and take photographs and had been caught by shell-fire with her two companions, and there were hundreds of others, Americans and Indians, New Zealanders and British, and many Germans too.

Just to the left of the road, about two hundred yards short of the main German position in the Hotel Continental, lay the ruins of a church and convent. In the crypt of this church was established the double battalion headquarters of the two battalions holding the left and centre sections of the town, namely the Grenadiers and the Coldstream. The Welsh Guards had their headquarters in the gaol, over to the right on the S. Pasquale road, and they were holding the right sector. The church was completely destroyed and lay in rubble fifteen feet thick on top of the crypt, which had been shored up and could stand a direct hit. The convent was a modern concrete building which had been very badly damaged but not completely destroyed by the bombing. It held the reserve Grenadier Company (No. 2, under David Bonsor), and could be reached by day with care.

In the crypt we lived a strange life entirely by artificial light. There were two entrances, the front door facing west towards the Germans and the back door being a very narrow hole through the rubble through which it was impossible to pass without divesting oneself of equipment, but which was not under observation and appeared to be much the safer of the two. Inside we lived in the bays of the crypt, one each for the battalion headquarters, one for the R.A.P., one for the pioneers who also did the cooking on a petrol cooker, one for the signallers and one for the Ayrshire Yeomanry O.P. There was also a small headquarters of some New Zealand tanks which had got stuck in their attack and were still being maintained in the town, so they could not be withdrawn.

Below ground there was no distinction between night and day, and the busy time was naturally during the night hours. We would get up and have breakfast just before midday, then our main meal would come about seven or eight o'clock in the evening, followed shortly by 'Exercise Flurry', as we called the nightly arrival of the porters with rations and stores. They would usually be clear by about midnight and the commanding officers would then go round the forward company headquarters, getting back to the crypt about two o'clock for a cup of tea, then bed for all except those on duty.

Many of the New Zealanders had remained with us for the first 24 hours and it was interesting to hear them sending signals in Maori. Nearly all signals and telephone messages could be picked up by the Germans, so we had to be cautious in our use of the telephone and could only call the forward platoons by blowing into the handset, as a turn of the handle would be as good as ringing up the Germans themselves. The Welsh Guards used to speak Welsh within the battalion, which foxed the Germans so well that they fired over pamphlets in Hindustani.

The New Zealanders were grand, but they used to swan about more than we did. One of them came in during the day with a cracked head caused by some falling bricks. A steel helmet had other uses than keeping off ricochets in Cassino. It was not possible to evacuate any but the most serious casualties in day time, so he waited in the R.A.P. till dark. As next day was Good Friday and I wanted to get round the 'A' echelons, I accompanied him to the A.D.S. The arrangement was to walk as far as the Bailey bridges and to ring up for a Jeep to meet us there, and it was reckoned that both parties ought to arrive at the same time so that there would be the minimum of hanging about in that unhealthy spot, but my New Zealander had no intention whatever of lingering anywhere on the mad mile, and led me at such a pace that I had the greatest difficulty in keeping up with him. We were over the bridge before there was any sign of the Jeep, but he wouldn't stop there and we were well down the road to the A.D.S. before the Jeep came tearing along like a wild cat, nor would it stop for us, so eventually it had to be recalled by a despatch rider.

Having deposited the casualty in the A.D.S., I called in at the next house where rear Bn. H.Q. was living, finding Bob Coates and Stephen Whitwell there. It was not a very quiet spot as it was right on the main Route 6 about a mile out of the town and got shelled quite a lot. They had to be just as close as we did during the day as it was under observation from the Monastery. Eventually I got back to 'A' Echelon at S. Pietro at about 4 a.m. on Good Friday. I had a short service during the morning for all who could come, about twenty including the Brigadier, but as it was impossible to have any of the Liturgy. I just read them the Passion according to St John and the Lamentations and heard confessions. That night I returned to the Crypt, going through the usual performance with the porter parties, but all was quiet except for the peculiar whistle of the smoke shells passing overhead and bursting with their soft crack. Next night, or rather on Easter Sunday morning, I went up to the forward companies with Colonel Hugh, No 2 (Ian Skimming) and No 3 (Desmond Chichester) and 'S' (Andrew Neilson). No. 3 had a horrible place where it was impossible to sit upright and the roof looked as if it might come down any moment.

The walk through that dead town in the dark, threading our way between the enormous bomb craters in single file and climbing over debris, with the awful smell of unburied dead everywhere, was one of the most nerve-racking experiences I ever had, and when we got back I found all my underclothes were wringing wet. I was determined to say an Easter Mass in Cassino somehow, and found a place in the convent occupied by the Grenadier Company next door. The 'altar' was a ledge six inches off the floor, and the congregation (only five could come) had to stand round, as all the rest of the floor space was filled with sleeping guardsmen who had just come off duty, but it was most consoling to all of us to have Mass and Holy Communion in such circumstances.

20 – SWANNERS' CHECK-POINT
Easter Sunday 9 April 1944

A curious incident occurred on Easter Sunday afternoon. Two American G.I.s came up in a Jeep from Naples, parked their Jeep at the Bailey bridge, and walked up into the town in broad daylight. They had imbibed freely, but the one that was less drunk thought he had gone far enough and stopped near the knocked-out tank. The other came past the Crypt and we shouted to him from the back door but he took no notice and walked on, making for the Hotel Continental. The Germans must have been asleep after their Easter dinner, as nothing happened till suddenly a sentry took a hurried shot at him as he stood swaying to and fro and looking about him and just grazed the back of his thighs, whereat he took to his heels and somehow managed to get away with it and get back with his friend to the A.D.S. After that a 'Swanners Check Post' was established behind Monte Trocchio to discourage unwanted visitors.

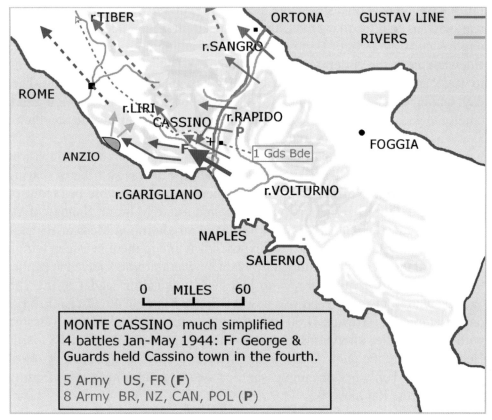

Cassino, the final break-through in May 1944

53

On the Monday the battle woke up again and there was some fairly heavy shelling and mortaring, but we lay very close and only one Grenadier was hit, a rather nasty chest wound and he was breathing through the hole. Elston sewed him up and we left him till the porters came and carried him back at night. I went with Colonel Johnny Goschen, who had taken over command of the Grenadiers when Colonel Algy got a Brigade, to see No. 3 Company (Stan Jameson), and later went to No. 2 (David Bonsor) who were in the convent next door and could be reached with care by day. The following night I went again with Colonel Johnny to see No. 1 Company (Pat Needham), who were out in the left sector on the road to the station, a better walk than to the Coldstream companies, but very smelly. On the following night, Thursday the 13th the battalion headquarters were relieved by the spare 'teams' and the Grenadier R.A.P. took over from us. The new Grenadier chaplain, Arthur Guthrie, came in, so I went out to make room for him. It was a pitch dark night and raining hard, so I stuck close to Bob Southey but had the misfortune to fall flat on my back in a shell-hole, not a very wet one luckily. Colonel Hugh was with us, not at all well as he was developing jaundice, and it was an unpleasant walk as both Baileys were out of action and we had to straddle sideways along the girders to get across the river. But it was better than having to wade, and we got back to 'A' Echelon at 4 a.m. on the Friday morning. That day, having checked up with the M.D.S., I went back to San Potito for a night, chiefly to get a wash and change of clothes, but returned next day to San Pietro as it was Saturday, in order to organise Sunday Masses.

That evening I went up to see the Coldstream reserve company which was in a farm on the east side of the Rapido. The family was still there, sharing the kitchen with the officers, the family sleeping in one double bed (four of them) and the three officers in another. I said a late Mass on Sunday at 'A' Echelon as most people were 'spark out', and an afternoon Mass at Brigade H.Q. in San Pasquale, and felt very exposed driving up there in a Jeep within full view of the Monastery, though I was told it was all right. I stayed to supper there and met Jocelyn Gurney who had been a squadron leader in the 2nd Welsh Guards at Codford and was now a Brigade Major in 4th Division. Next day I returned to Brigade H.Q., dined with them, and walked into Cassino with the Brigadier afterwards along the other road to see the Welsh Guards Headquarters in the gaol. This was a much more covered approach for most of the way and only became unpleasant for the last quarter mile, after fording a branch of the Rapido.

The supplies on this route were also much more easily worked, as the Jeeps could get right up to a quarry on the outskirts of the town and it was a very short carry from there. The gaol was a very strong building with thick walls, much damaged by missiles. We got in and out without harm and Colonel David Block, who commanded the Ayrshire Yeomanry, drove me home to San Pietro in his Jeep. I remember him commenting with pride on the lovely sharp crack which his beloved 25 pounders made when they fired, a noise that I found some difficulty in admiring cordially. The next day I took a day off and went to the dentist!

During the rest of that week I contented myself with a visit to rear Battalion H.Q. on the Wednesday, at a time when the Germans decided to shell the area, a visit to the Crypt on Thursday night, coming back with Bill Corbould and two other walking wounded, and another trip to the rear H.Q. on the Saturday with the relieving party of the 6th Black Watch. I watched the relief till midnight, the only incident being that David Chetwode and Dicky Paget-Cooke and I got caught by some shelling near Pastinelle while trying to tow away a couple of abandoned Jeeps, and got back to San Pietro at 2 a.m. but was no sooner in bed than my tent blew away. The whole Brigade was out of Cassino on the 22nd, and so our first tour of duty there came to an end. All were very tired, so there were not many at Mass on the Sunday.

I went to 2 AGRA Headquarters at Aquafondate on the Sunday night and spent Monday with Larry Twomey, whose Medium regiment was engaged in the battle towards the north of Cassino. I returned to San Potito that night and found the Brigade settled down for a few days rest, so I asked for and obtained three days leave. Calling at various hospitals on the way, I managed to see Colonel Hugh, Dick Alderson, Taffy Howard-Stepney, John Henry Lambert and David Noel, and spent the first night with Fr Paulinus Angold (Buckfast) at 92 General Hospital, Naples. Next day I went on to Cava de Tirreni, having a look at Pompeii ruins and basilica on the way. At the Abbey I received a true Benedictine welcome and was very glad to have 36 hours rest there. Abbot Rea (now Abbot of Monte Cassino) was most charming and so were all the others, and we managed to converse in French or Latin, though not as fluently as I would have liked. I had to leave early on Saturday morning in order to get back for the Sunday, travelling by way of Salerno, Avellino and Caserta so completing the circuit of Vesuvius. Most of the Brigade were at Mass on the Sunday, it being very convenient to have them so concentrated.

Being due for typhus and T.A.B. inoculations I duly received these and took it easy for twenty four hours. On Wednesday May 3rd there was a

Chaplains' conference at the seminary in Piedemonte d'Alife, and next day we took the road for Cassino once more. After a night at San Pietro we went into the town again on the night of the 5th, a mercifully quiet journey in bright moonlight. As the next day was Saturday I had to do the Mad Mile again that night, as it was no use staying in for the Sunday and I could do more good at 'A' Echelon, but I returned on the Sunday night, walking in with Ronnie Furze, the third night running, but all was quiet. I stayed in the crypt for 48 hours, only going to the convent next door to see No. 2 Coy of the Grenadiers (Joshua Rowley), and on the Tuesday night I walked out with Ian Skimming. That night Sharp, who had taken over Eddie Trafford's platoon in 'S' Coy, was killed. At this time of year there were many fireflies about, and in the prevailing tension this resulted in many wild goose chases after supposed collaborators signalling to the Monastery. There were also innumerable frogs whose croaking sounded appallingly loud in that eerie stillness, and our smoke shells always charmed the nightingales into song. Even the horrors of the battle field could not get the better of the birds and beasts.

Next day I went down to the I.R.T.D. just past the Caudine Forks in the hopes of seeing Fr Vincent Cavanagh, but he was out. I did see Eustace Montagu, however, just back from the 5th Battalion Grenadiers in Anzio, and Taffy Howard Stepney in hospital on my way back. I also went up to the rear battalion H.Q. during the night.

21 – THE LIRI CROSSING
11 May 1944

The big battle to force the Liri crossing started next day, May 11th, at 11p.m. with a barrage of 1200 guns. [This was the fourth & final battle of Monte Cassino: much of VIII Army was 'borrowed' for it from the east side of Italy. The key fighting (and credit) was on the part of the French and the Poles.] It did not sound like a very big bombardment from where we were, as the gun positions were so blanketed from each other by hills. All the infantry fighting was to the south of us, and we were told only to pin down the Paratroops in the town as far as possible until the 4th Division had cut the road to the west of them and the Poles had captured the Monastery. The town was therefore fairly quiet, and when I walked up with Dick Alderson and the porters on the night of the 12th we had a peaceful journey both ways. Next day I visited the mortars and machine guns of support company with Bob Clive and David Toler in Bob's Jeep. On Sunday the 14th, after usual morning Masses, I went up again with Dick to the Crypt. Dick was night blind and had been starting off earlier and earlier, and this time we were really rather foolish as we reached the telephone kiosk in broad daylight, despite the smoke. I did not stay in, as the Crypt was rather full, so next day went down to the hospitals at Caserta and Cancello to see the wounded. At Cancello I saw Colonel Poston, my old commanding officer of 97 General Hospital.

The following night, the 16th, I went up with Dick again and also managed to get forward to No.2 and 'S' companies. The Germans were reacting more that night – probably they were thinning out their troops – and we got shelled on the way home, two shells landing uncomfortably close. On the 17th I made my last trip into Cassino, the sixteenth time. I had done the Mad Mile, and my luck held, as all was quiet. The really sticky job at Cassino was undoubtedly that of the porters who took in the supplies. It was interesting again to compare the different methods adopted by the battalions. The Grenadiers kept the number of porters to the absolute minimum, but loaded them so heavily that if a man fell down he could not get up again unaided. The Coldstream took more men, less heavily loaded and more mobile. Both Battalions were lucky in having practically no casualties among their porters. Victor Cubitt did the lion's share of portering for the Grenadiers. I think he covered the Mad Mile more than forty times. Dick Alderson did most of ours, though of course others took a turn off these two now and again. We had very few casualties in the town on the whole, though there were some unfortunate incidents. Drill-Sergeant Walker showed himself at a window for less than thirty seconds one day and was killed by a sniper, and a heavy shell fired at the Castle detonated a box of 36 Grenades inside with some fatal results, but we were not so unfortunate as the 6th Black Watch, who had a section post wiped out by bazookas one night.

Cassino fell on the 18th when the 4th Division and the Poles joined up on Route Six west of the town. Unfortunately we got but few prisoners, as the Germans had been able to get the bulk of the garrison away during the preceding nights when it became plain that the town could not be held. The Brigade was accordingly withdrawn to a concentration area just east of the town, ready to take up the pursuit, with the rest of 6th Armoured Division which had now been moved up. The battle had been raging for a week, and the Liri had been forced by 8th Indian and 4th Divisions with the Canadian and 78th Divisions following up. The fight had moved some miles west to the Adolf Hitler line that ran across Aquino airport and for some days we had to wait for the situation to be cleared up in that area.

22 – THE RAPIDO CROSSING
19 May 1944

On the 19th we moved across the Rapido by one of the assault bridges at S Angelo in Teodice. This village had been in the midst of the fiercest fighting and the devastation was as bad as Cassino. The weather had broken, as usual after a heavy bombardment, though the scientists say that it is not caused by the guns. We advanced a considerable distance on the far side of the river and had just gone into harbour when we were told that we had gone much too far, were in fact right on the edge of Aquino airport, and were told to come back again as quickly as possible, which we lost no time in doing. Our new harbour area was not far from Pignataro in very close country, and unfortunately just in front of a battery of medium guns, so there was not much peace and quiet. We remained in that place for the next five days, unscathed by the enemy but Elston's driver, Gdsn Walker, was badly hit in the arm by a premature from the battery just behind us.

On the 24th the Canadians broke through the Hitler line and took Aquino, not without heavy losses particularly in tanks. The Germans A/T guns were very cleverly concealed in standing corn, and I had the impression of seeing about forty or fifty burnt-out tanks in front of them. We did a night move on the 25th in order to pass through the Canadians and force the crossing of the Melfa river, and suffered a rather sharp air attack brought on by some Canadians 'brewing-up' in the dark. I suppose they had forgotten the existence of the Luftwaffe, which proceeded to give us an unpleasant time with A.P. bombs and H.E. by the light of blazing vehicles. The Welsh Guards had a number of casualties but we were luckier and had none.

Friday 26th brought another very slow approach march while the Melfa was being forced, but we put the river behind us in the evening. The Germans were now fighting a rearguard action on the high ground covering Arce and we continued to press them back with Route 6 as our axis. The Welsh Guards were in the lead, supported by the 17/21st Lancers, and were having a sticky time. I got word that Christopher Maude had been killed, a direct hit by an eight-inch shell on his slit trench, so I went up forward on foot to bury him. It was just a case of filling in the trench and saying the burial service over it, as there was not much left of any of them, poor fellows. Robert Cobbold, Pat Bankier, and Tim Hayley were also killed that day [*vere* 27th]. As the advance was being well held it was decided to take the high ground on the left of the main road by a night attack. There were two hills, Monte Piccolo and Monte

58

'The old walled town of Perugia': this engraving is of Urbino, captured by the 4th Indian Division in August, when their I.O. Capt. Magrath walked in, sent by the Brigadier, as he was fluent in Italian to see if any of the enemy were present. They were not: but the Mayor entertained him to lunch . The engraving is a gift of the Urbino Commune.

PRAYERS FOR A BURIAL

Often I was asked to bury non-Catholics, and puzzled as to what form would be best to use, until I got this out of a L.O.C.K. magazine from Michael Hollings, which I then used habitually for this purpose:

I am the Resurrection and the Life: he that believeth in Me, though he be dead, shall live.

Let us pray.

Be kind, O Lord, to this Thy son who has come into Thy presence and forgive him all his sins, because, whatever wrong he may have done, You know he did believe and trust in You. **Amen.**

> Eternal rest give unto him, O Lord
>
> **And let perpetual light shine upon him**.
>
> Lord have mercy on him.
>
> **Christ have mercy on him**.
>
> Lord have mercy on him.

**Our Father . . .   And lead us not into temptation:
But deliver us from evil. Amen.**

Let us pray.

O God, loving and merciful, while we here bury the body of this Thy son, do Thou receive his soul into everlasting peace. **Amen.**

I am the Resurrection and the Life: he that believeth in Me, though he be dead, shall live.

May his soul and the souls of all the faithful departed,, through the mercy of God, rest in peace. **Amen.**

Pause here for a few moments' silent prayer.

And now, O Lord, remember us, who leave our comrade in Thy care; give us grace to lead a good and holy life, so that, whenever our time comes, we may be ready. **Amen.**

Grande, which covered the main road where it took a sharp right angled bend between Arce and Ceprano, so if these hills could be taken the whole rearguard position would collapse.

There was very little time for reconnaissance before nightfall and the attack was timed for midnight. A barrage was put down on the crests of the hills and the Germans employed their usual tactics of withdrawing down the far slope, leaving only a few men in observation, so when the attack went in the Coldstream on the right had little difficulty in gaining the summit of Monte Piccolo, though the enemy was very far from beaten yet. The Grenadiers were not so fortunate and were only partially successful in occupying the bigger Monte Grande. Then the Germans counter-attacked and dislodged one company of Grenadiers so dawn found us holding half the objective and the Germans the other half. All next day, Whitsunday May 28th, they continued to shell and counter-attack us. We had a combined R.A.P. in a farm house for the two battalions and dealt with a continual stream of wounded. Tony Way was very badly wounded in the stomach during the night, and at various times during the day Michael Cooper, Jack Harkness, Bob Murdoch, Ian Skimming and Ray Crouch all passed through our hands wounded. Hugh Spencer and Bridgeman, subalterns in 3 and 'S' Companies were killed and Andrew Neilson was slightly wounded in the arm but refused to be evacuated. 'S' Company and No. 3 did a great job on Monte Piccolo and deserved most of the credit for the battle. Andrew got a D.S.O. and Desmond Chichester & Hugo Charteris, the M.C. During the afternoon I walked up to the Grenadiers and saw Victor Cubitt, Tom Faber and the remnants of Tony Way's Company. Just as I left them the Germans put down a heavy stonk on the area, and when I got back to the R.A.P. I found them bringing in Tom with a very bad wound in the back. The doctors would not touch him but evacuated him to a surgical team straight away. I anointed him before he went, whereat he recovered consciousness and seemed quite calm and happy. He stood the journey well and, though very ill for over a year, has made a good recovery. Tony Way also weathered the storm, though we never expected to see either of them alive again.

23 – THE WALK ROUND ROME
29 May 1944

The Germans withdrew during the night and we got the next day to sort ourselves out and bury our dead. The Grenadiers and Coldstream each had about 100 casualties, and we made a big graveyard in an orchard and brought in all the bodies from the three battalions to it. In the evening we held a combined burial service, the Anglican and non-Conformist one first followed by mine, and then the graves were filled in. We remained in the area for two more days, then advanced about five miles to a concentration area near Ceprano. Thence we struck off into the hills to the right of the main road and did a long night move starting at midnight of June 1/2nd and finishing at 7.30 a.m. near Alatri. Next day we moved again and reached a small village near Fumone where we bivouaced for the night. We were not in touch with the enemy at this time. Next day was Trinity Sunday, and as there was every prospect of continuing our advance I said Mass at 6.30 a.m. on the tail-board of my truck. The villagers were busy fetching their animals out of the caves where they had hidden them from the Germans, who were living on the country, while they were in retreat, but as soon as they saw me vested and ready to begin they left what they were doing and stood in a big semi-circle round the truck following the Mass with great devotion, a touching exhibition of their peasant faith.

We were then told we would not move that day, so I walked with Elston into Fumone, a small town perched on top of a hill, and in the afternoon we all went and bathed in the Lago di Canterno 'under the Porcian height'. A long and slow night move brought us to near Genazzano on the morning of the 6th, the day that Rome fell and the invasion of Normandy began. [*vere* Rome, 4th; Normandy 6th.] The R.A.F. must have caught a German convoy using this secondary road parallel to Route 6, for there were burnt-out German vehicles every few hundred yards for miles. On the 6th we moved slowly along past Palaestrina and turned off to by-pass Rome by the east. We followed for some miles an old and very rough Roman road, the Via Prenestina, paved apparently with the same stones that the Romans had laid when they made it. After a short halt on a big farm outside Rome we moved again through some suburbs and came out in an enormous stubble field on the banks of the Tiber about ten miles north east of the city. From here we could see the dome of St Peter's but not much else. The enemy appeared to have withdrawn into the hills east of Tivoli or away to the other side of the Tiber.

After a peaceful night I said Mass for the Coldstream, as it was Corpus Christi (June 8th) and had hardly finished before we were moved again. Our axis was now Route 4, the Via Salaria. A main railway runs parallel to the road and everywhere there was evidence of the great destruction done by the bombers, shattered engines, trucks and carriages and broken rails. The Welsh Guards had run into a German reaguard at Monterotondo and Colonel David

Davies-Scourfield had been wounded in the leg. Command devolved upon Colonel Jocelyn Gurney, who continued in command for nearly a year. About this time too, Colonel John Nelson arrived to take over the 3rd Grenadiers. He had been one of Colonel Algy's company commanders in Africa, and he too held his command till the following March.

We continued our advance at 4.30 a.m. on the 9th, leaving the main road and following the left bank of the Tiber towards Terni. The Germans made a determined effort to hold us at the crossing of the Farfa river and gave us a bad time for a whole day as they had many guns and nebelwerfers, and unlimited ammunition, the area being one of their big dumps. The R.A.P. was in a quarry at the top of a hill, and during the morning I walked forward to Battalion H.Q. to find out the news. On my return I found them all lying very close, as a German gun had found them and given them a good plastering, knocking out the American ambulance. Elston and I found a safer place behind a large tumulus and we were not much troubled again. I found seven holes in the body of my truck afterwards, but luckily no vital part was hit. During the afternoon a sharp action took place on a bound called 'Cicely Courtneidge', and battalion headquarters was unfortunately shelled out, all the officers becoming casualties except Robin Muir. Colonel Hugh Norman was badly hit in the leg, and so was Dick Chaplin, the adjutant. Bob Clive was slightly hit and Dick Alderson killed with a dozen men. We buried them near the R.A.P. and Colonel Bob Coates came up to take over command, making the third new commanding officer in the Brigade within the week.

Next day we continued the advance, out of touch with the enemy, by way of Poggio Mirteto station on the Tiber and Stimigliano to a pine wood just short of Narni, where we bivouaced for two days. From there we moved across the Tiber to the right bank and were directed on Perugia. The enemy held us up at S. Fortunato about 3 miles south of the town on the night of June 18th, and during the night George Lascelles was wounded and made prisoner while on patrol. The Germans then withdrew to the hills north of the town and we moved in on the 20th. Andy Angus and Henry Lumley-Savile were wounded when their Jeep went up on a mine just outside the town.

We were now faced with formidable hills again and our advance came to a stop for the time being, but we had every reason to be satisfied with an advance of two hundred miles in a month

24 – PERUGIA
20 June 1944

The next phase of the campaign was almost a return to the static warfare of the winter. The Germans appeared to have recovered themselves and to be prepared to dispute our further passage through the mountains north of Perugia, and we had to return to the methods of set-piece attacks on his position, taking one hill after another and always finding more beyond. For the next fortnight all three battalions were in the line, the Welsh Guards on Monte Malbe to the west, the Coldstream on Monte Pacciano due north of the town, and the Grenadiers on Monte Bagnolo to the east of them. The old walled town of Perugia was under observation from the German positions and they shelled it nearly every day, not indiscriminately but mostly in the station area. If they had known that practically every tank in the division was parked in the main square being frantically maintained after the long journey from Cassino, they might have shelled us a lot more. Coldstream battalion headquarters was in an old gate-house in the walls and the R.A.P. was close behind. I spent a fairly quiet week, as it was difficult to get to the battalions by day.

There was a fairly constant stream of casualties, and we lost Peter Gale killed and John Lumley wounded. Then on June 27th Victor Cubitt was killed. He had gone up to visit battalion headquarters for orders about his A/T platoon which was billeted in the town, and volunteered to help somebody who was digging a slit trench, as there had been some fairly heavy stonking. A shell caught him as he was working above ground and killed him outright. Victor was really irreparable loss to me, and I missed him very badly, as did very many other people, not only in his own battalion but in the whole of the Brigade. His platoon worshipped him and would do anything for him. I buried him the same day in a military cemetery under the shadow of the great Benedictine church of S. Pietro, and came away feeling the world to be a much poorer place. God rest him.

The same day I went up to No. 3 Company on a call from Desmond Chichester to bury seven men who had been killed. None of them were Catholics, and the message had really been sent to Jones-Davis of the Welsh Guards, but somehow got repeated to me; he arrived just after I had finished and I walked back with him, calling on the way at battalion headquarters which had moved forward to a large farm in the foot-hills. The town being no longer under observation, we had moved into a large and luxurious villa just outside which was said to belong to a prominent local Fascist. Certainly his wife and

63

family did not receive us with any marked cordiality at first, though relations improved with time. The Welsh Guards also had an excellent mess in a luxury that we had never before seen in Italy. There was a large chocolate factory in which the Field Ambulance was established, and I was given a box of chocolate bars which I strongly suspected of being loot, but salved my conscience by giving most of them away to Italian kiddies. It was not very good chocolate anyway.

Camp 1934: Miles Fitzalan-Howard, John Gilbey,Edward Grieve, Michael Fitzalan-Howard – future Captains & more.

Those who trained them, Capt.Boyan, Maj.Forbes, Ampleforth OTC

25 – VISITING ASSISI
29 June 1944

On June 29th I went with Colonel Sandy Sangster in his Jeep to look at Assisi, and we were both tremendously impressed so much so that I returned the same afternoon in my own truck and took Michael Hollings. We concentrated on the three [*sic*] churches, of St Francis' Basilica, and the Portiuncula chapel at S. Maria degli Angeli, hoping to return later and see it more thoroughly, a disappointed hope. Assisi had been marvellously preserved from the war. The Germans made it a hospital town and the commandant had been an excellent Catholic who would not allow any damage or looting. Only the railway station, some distance away on the plain, had been bombed, and in their advance the 8th Indian Division had not been compelled to fight for the town, so it was spared all shelling. St Francis had surely kept it under his protection.

There were High Mass and Vespers in the Basilica, it being the feast of SS Peter and Paul, beautifully sung by the only good choir I ever heard in Italy. Most of the Italian singing sounded appallingly harsh and untuneful to our ears, especially the voices of the children, which one would expect to be sweet and true.

About this time we were having a certain amount of trouble over men going absent from the line, 'doing a nip' as they called it. There was no problem of this kind in the 1914 war, as the penalty was death then, and it was enforced, but this penalty was abolished in 1936, with the result that the bad man was quite prepared to face a term of imprisonment of not more than five years, but more often two and commuted at that, in order to save his life or even only to get away from the discomforts of the line. The death penalty did not keep the good man there, for he stayed of his own accord so the only ones who benefitted by the abolition of the penalty were the bad men. I had a go at persuading some of them to go back and accept another chance, but with no success. They would not face the others who had stayed there. The position was not improved by tales, no doubt exaggerated, of men who had been picked up by the military police and sentenced by court-martial, living safely in easy jobs down at Naples with few apparent restrictions on their liberty. On the other hand one could thank God that the great majority did stick it month after month and year after year, all honour to them.

Our next move took place as usual on a Sunday, July 2nd, and we halted for two days at Castiglion Fosco, where I was able to arrange a Mass for the whole Brigade on the Monday. On the Wednesday we moved up the west side of 'reedy Trasimene', the main road running along the lake shore close to the main line railway on which several trains had been wrecked by the R.A.F. and were strewn in the fields on either side. We stopped for the night in a very poor and dirty village called Borghetto and moved on next day to Camucia, an industrial suburb of Cortona situated at the foot of the hill 'from where Cortona lifts to heaven her diadem of towers' [Macaulay, *Horatius*, 'Lars Porsena of Clusium, by the Nine Gods he swore...']. Here we stayed for about a week, and I paid a hurried visit to Cortona with Elston but we were not much impressed with anything except the view. Fr Dommersen and I were able to lay on a big Mass on the Sunday for the divisional troops in the new church of Christ the King at Camucia. We filled the church with about three hundred men, which greatly impressed the young parish priest, who told me that all the time the Germans were there he never saw a single German at any service, though individuals would creep in to church sometimes to say their prayers when nobody was about.

There was much active preparation going on for the forcing of the gap in the hills south of Arezzo, one of the historical battle-fields of Italy. It was a full scale attack very carefully laid on, and all company commanders were flown over the position in Taylorcraft first. The attack went in on the 15th, after a very long and slow all-night approach march to S. Andrea. The Coldstream attacked on the right with the Grenadiers, under Colonel John Nelson who had just returned, on the left, and gained the high ground and their objectives at Stoppeacci and Marsupino [*sic* but unknown to our maps or Google.] after a fairly sharp action. There were not many casualties but unfortunately we lost Andrew Neilson who was commanding 'S' Company. He stepped on a Schu mine which blew off his foot and he died the next day.

The R.A.P. was called forward in the afternoon to Stoppeacci, which we reached after a very steep and hot climb of about a thousand feet under the blazing July sun and carrying all our kit. We were nearly exhausted on arrival, but found several wounded to attend to, including Hugo Charteris. The Welsh Guards passed through us and occupied the defile on the main road south of Arezzo during the night. The Germans promptly evacuated the town and continued their withdrawal down the Arno valley. Next day we collected the dead and I buried them all together, mostly Scots Guards, and the Scots Guards piper played *The Flowers of the Forest* after the funeral. The action took place on a Sunday as usual, July 16th, and next day we were withdrawn to billets at S. Andrea in a large farm house with a private chapel in it, much to my satisfaction.

26 – THE ARNO VALLEY
17 July 1944

Nearly all the big farm-houses had a private chapel, built so far as I could judge in the 17th or early 18th centuries, and some of them had a Papal privilege of reserving the Blessed Sacrament, even though they were within a few minutes' walk of the Parish Church. It was delightful to find such facilities available, and only distressing to see how little such privileges were appreciated by the inhabitants. As a rule only the women-folk showed any interest.

During the next few days the troops were slowly filtering through the Olmo gap and Arezzo and taking up the pursuit down the Arno valley. I went in to Arezzo one day, and lunched with Pete Crowder at Eighth Army H.Q. in the hills south of Arezzo, on another. On July 22nd we were moved to a new area at S. Leo west of Arezzo at the end of the week, and I managed to get the Church, which had been badly hit by shell-fire, ready for Mass on the Sunday with the aid of Sgt Green, who was much impressed by the fact that a statue of Our Lady in a glass case was undamaged, though the whole of the wall was pitted with shell splinters. Another move followed on the Monday, July 24th, to a place called Ponticino, where we were billeted in a farm. Here we got orders for Exercise 'Roger', which turned out to be an inspection by H.M. the King.

I was detailed to be one of the Brigade representatives to be presented to His Majesty. On July 26th it meant a very early move, reveille at 0245 hours, and we were in position lining a road at L'Olmo before the King arrived at 0830 hours. When we got back we were moved again to the right bank of the Arno nearly opposite Montevarchi. The battalion was not actually in contact with the enemy, but we were within artillery range, and had the odd casualty from shell fire every day. The battalion was dispersed among the most lovely peach orchards. It was a shame to have to drive one's truck under the trees, knocking off half-ripe peaches which would have cost a fortune in London.

There had been another change of chaplains in the Armoured Brigade, as Father Alban Boultwood O.S.B. had gone sick. He was replaced by Father Nicholas Holman O.S.B. (Downside). We also had a change of Brigadier. Charles Haydon left us, to everyone's regret, to go to the Joint Planning Staff in Washington. He was relieved by another 'Mick', Andrew Montagu-Douglas-Scott, whom I met several times while he was commanding the 1st Irish Guards (July 30th). He had come back to the Regiment

Typical battle ground in central Italy

from the reserve in 1939 and was the only officer, so far as I know, who commanded every formation from a Platoon to a Corps during the war. He was a splendid person, and brought with him to Bde HQ as M.T.O. another great character, Big Jim Egan. Both remained with us till the reorganisation of March 1945.

The first few days of August brought some very unpleasant fighting as we gradually pressed the German rear-guards down the Arno valley. For one thing there was the great heat, and for another the state of the tracks, which were churned into white dust, and all movements of transport had to be at a crawl in low gear, because, as the signs at the roadside put it, 'Dust Means Death' . The enemy resisted largely by harassing shell fire, and the country was the most puzzling that I have ever seen for finding one's way about, so that all 'bounds' were marked by Provost by sign-boards bearing the names of public schools. Ampleforth was one of the bounds, but I never actually passed it, or I would have pinched the board as a souvenir!

We moved into the lead on August 1st near Figline Valdarno and for the next week fought our way forward against stiffish resistance. On the 5th and 6th we were in a village called Cancelli, the RAP established in the Doctor's house, which we failed to observe was on a cross-roads well registered by the German guns. The result was a direct hit on the house, the shell penetrating the wall just opposite where I was standing. Luckily no one was hurt, though we were all shaken. I spent the rest of the day being bomb-happy in my truck. We had Peter Perrott and Brian Rudd killed here, and Raoul Robin wounded. The village was gradually pounded to bits by the German shells, and there were still a lot of civilians living in the cellars, including the priest, who, poor man, went out every now and again to see how much more damage had been done to his church. There was little left of it by the time we moved on. Our next move was to an enormous old castle called the Villa Bensi. In the immense cellars under the house there were about 200 Italian civilians living among the vast vats of wine. It was the safest shelter I have ever seen.

Our next headquarters was a large and hideous house called San Mezzano, built like a Moorish palace by some eccentric. It had been used by the Germans as a hospital, which perhaps explained why they never shelled it, though it was a most conspicuous land mark perched on the top of a hill. It smelt awfully of wounded Germans, a curiously characteristic odour which we encountered many times.

Ian Fraser came to join 'S' Company while we were at San Mezzano, also the 7th R.B. came up quite close behind us and I saw Clive Conlin several times. He was badly wounded in the leg about a month later. The battalion was pressing forward all the time, though rather slowed up by the rain, clearing the foothills of the Prato Magno, the massif on the right bank of the Arno. At last, on August 18th, came the order for the Brigade to pull out and rest at Renacci, half way back to Arezzo. It was the first time the whole Brigade had been out of action together since landing in Italy, and full use was taken of the opportunity to send everyone on leave to Rome.

27 – LEAVE IN ROME
August 1944

I took the road south after my Sunday Masses on August 20th and travelled via Cortona, Orvieto and Viterbo, reaching Rome in 6½ hours, a journey of 180 miles. We had a camp in Mussolini's sports arena near the Milvian Bridge, and as I wanted my driver, Paddy Gavin, to be free, I decided not to use my truck. As it was August and the trams were impossibly crowded, I regretted this decision before very long. On the first day, having bought a map of Rome and refused a pamphlet entitled *1500 Years of History in 35 Minutes*, I managed to visit St Peter's, the Forum and the Colosseum, finishing up at St Paul's. I arranged to stay here for three nights – not a good place, as it is too low-lying and stiflingly hot at that time of year, and trekked all the way back to the camp for my kit, but was lucky enough to borrow a Jeep for the return journey.

Night brought little relief from the heat, and there were many mosquitos and no nets. Next day I was feeling really knocked-up with the heat, so confined my attentions to the Basilica. I said Mass at St Paul's tomb on two days. Next day, feeling rather better, I had lunch at the Ambasciatore with Fr Humphrey Bright, S.C.F. Italy (now Aux. Bp of Birmingham), and met Jim Utley there, with whom I dined that night. I also went to St Mary Major during the day, and on the following morning to a public audience at the Vatican. An official passed me through the ropes to the steps of the throne, and after a long wait the Holy Father was carried in. He makes a great impression on everyone, Catholic and Protestant, who go to these daily audiences, which he is continuing throughout the summer. He spoke from the throne, first in French then in rather stilted but idiomatic English. Then he came down and talked to each of us who were inside the ring. He blessed some Rosaries for me, and I was thrilled to have spoken to both the Pope and the King within a month.

In the afternoon Paddy brought my truck to S. Paolo and we set off for Subiaco. There was not much sign of war damage along the forty miles of road through Tivoli until we reached the town of Subiaco itself, which had been very heavily bombed by the Americans. We went on to St Scholastica's Abbey and were met by an English priest, an oblate of the Order, who was normally M.C. in Florence Cathedral, but had been forced to retire to Subiaco to evade the Germans. With him I climbed up the hill to the upper Monastery of the Sacro Speco. It was a great contrast and joy to find this other shrine of St Benedict completely unscathed by the war. I spent some time n the sacred cave itself, and would have liked to have spent longer, as it was refreshingly cool up there after the sweltering heat of the Campagna. We returned to Rome in the evening, and next morning, after a hurried visit to St John Lateran, we returned to Renacci by way of Bolsena and Siena, a seven hours journey.

Major-General H Murray came to see the Battalion on assuming command of 6th Armoured Division. He is a Cameronian who had commanded a Brigade in the 51st Highland Division at the time of the Sicily landings, and looked rather like Mr Punch; we called him the Professor, for some reason or other.

All this week we were kept hanging about in the Arno valley, waiting for a move which never came. One night the Luftwaffe suddenly livened things up by dropping A.P. bombs and Sgt O'Rourke was wounded. He had been given the M.M. in Africa, and he never came back to us.

28 – THE GOTHIC LINE
2 September 1944

On Sept 2nd the move came at last, to Consuma, a summer health resort of the Florentines, some 2000 feet up on the Prato Magno. The enemy had now been pushed back across the Sieve and Florence had been entered from the south. Every house in Consuma was booby-trapped, with the usual unfortunate results to the returning civilians. A woman brought a little boy, who had been injured by a booby trap, for treatment at the R.A.P. She was in great distress, and when we assured her that he was not badly hurt, 'It is not him', she said 'it's the other three; they have all been killed.'

A tremendous rainstorm in the night bogged down all the trucks, so it was just as well we were not engaging the enemy. Since Cassino we have come forward 330 miles, about 50 of them fighting forward on foot. Casualties to the Brigade since landing in Italy have been 82 officers and 1100 other ranks. The Grenadier Guards band has been touring the area, giving concerts. Sandy Hogarth, who was a subaltern in the 3rd Bn Windsor in 1922, brought them out, but unfortunately he fell ill and died in Rome, and so I never saw him.

The Welsh Guards were occupying a hamlet which was the scene of one of the few authentic atrocities that we came across. The Germans, apparently criminal lunatics, had herded the harmless villagers in a farm-yard and machine-gunned them before leaving. They also left other unmentionable traces of their occupation behind. After a week in the Consuma area we moved to near Dicomano, about fifteen miles up the river Sieve, and the Brigade was flung in to the assault on the Gothic line. The main attack was up the Forli road towards the pass through the Alpe di S Benedetto above S. Godenzo. We were put in on the left of the road up in the foothills, and attacked Monte Peschiena, a 3500 foot mountain which dominated the road from that side. On the day before the battle I managed a trip into Florence, which was getting organised as the principal winter leave centre on the west of the Apennines. It might well have been the only chance of visiting it; little did we think that we should go there many times during the next seven months.

The battle was a slow matter of climbing great hills and driving in what was little more than token resistance. I made one trip up to Tac H.Q. with Bob Clive up a very bad Jeep track, and eventually moved up to them by a rather better side road to a place called Villore.

There was a chaplains' conference at the Jesuit house in Florence on Monday Sept 18th, and after attending it I returned to F2 Echelon at Vicchio to find all packed up and ready to move. It was the old 'Plumbers' role of stopping a gap on Tenth Corps front, and entailed a long drive in two stages, up the Arno to Arezzo and then north to near Laverna, the Monte Alverna where St Francis of Assisi received the Stigmata. The Franciscan monastery was in German hands and we had unfortunately to put a few shells into it before they would let go, without much harm being done. My truck got ditched just as we arrived and had to be pulled out by a carrier. I chiefly remember that it was a very wet night and that several shells passed over us, the consequent mental struggle as to whether to remain in bed in the truck or to seek safety in the wet underneath being eventually decided in favour of the former.

I was able to visit the monastery next day, as the Germans had pulled out. Our services were no longer necessary, so we moved back to near Arezzo. Here I got word that the Lovat Scouts would be glad to see a priest, so I went up to them at Sansepolcro. I found Andrew Macdonald in command of H.Q. Squadron. Sandy Fraser was commanding No. 1 Squadron, but they were detached some way off and I did not see him. I had already arranged to say Masses for 2 AGRA, the Coldstream, the Welsh Guards & the Ayrshire Yeomanry on the Sunday, Monday and Tuesday so had to get one of the 10th Corps chaplains to see to the Scouts. They had been trained as mountaineers in the Canadian Rockies and were now maintaining touch across the Appenines between Eighth Army and Fifth Army. On the Wednesday we moved back to our old area at Piaccetto, near Pontassieve. It was quite close to Vallombrosa and I would have liked to have visited the Benedictine Monastery there, but was told the road was mined.

29 – MOUNTAINS IN WINTER
From October 1944

So ended September and the summer campaign of movement. The next six months brought us a spell of static infantry mountain warfare up a very poor maintenance route in quite appalling winter conditions. The main Gothic line had been broken completely and the Germans had withdrawn to the northern slopes of the Apennines. Here they had all the advantages of ground, with short, easy, covered supply lines, while we were left with nearly fifty miles of inferior and badly damaged roads over a high pass and down a precipitous valley.

The only decent high road ran over the Futa Pass and was within the American sector, and British trucks were not allowed to so much as show their radiators on it, with the exception of ambulances and 'starred' cars. This meant, not only that we had an extremely poor road to carry all the traffic for two divisions, but it was so narrow that traffic could only flow one way. For four hours traffic could move north from Scarperia, then the road would be closed for two hours, by which time the lorries were reckoned to have got somewhere near Castle del Rio. The southbound traffic was then released and flowed south for four hours, and so on. During the night the road was closed entirely for some hours maintenance. The effect of this was that if you started out from Florence you might be lucky and get a straight run through, or you might be held up for six hours while the traffic flowed the other way, which was quite maddening. It was almost an impossibility to get there and back in one day.

Then the road itself was only designed for light agricultural traffic. Our heavy lorries soon broke the surface to bits, and not only were all the bridges blown, but also many of the corners in the pass, where the road overhung a sheer drop of several hundred feet. The Sappers worked many miracles in making it passable to vehicles at all, and the Pioneers, mostly Basutos who had never seen snow before, did prodigious work on the whole length of the surface in the teeth of the severest winter weather. During the winter months I gave up in despair taking my truck over the pass. I used to take it as far as Scarperia, where the one-way traffic began and the ominous notice 'Chains' was so often displayed, going round the long detour by Pontassieve and Dicomano rather than by the bad direct road; from Scarperia I used then to hitch-hike up to Brigade H.Q., having sent the truck back to the rest area at

Strada in Chianti. Coming down again I could not order the truck to meet me at Scarperia, so it meant hitch-hiking the whole way, about 70 miles.

In the first week of October a situation arose which demanded our immediate and rapid return to the sector of the front north of Florence. The American division which had broken through the Gothic line near Firenzuola had been met by Italian partisans who informed them that they were holding the 'castle' on Monte Battaglia and implored their aid. A Brigade of the U.S. 88th Division (the Blue Devils) was sent forward to occupy this important key point, a mountain some 2500 feet high crowned by the ruins of a castle which was a landmark for miles around. This caused a salient deep into the German lines, and the position was almost entirely surrounded by Germans except for the very precarious track which ran up to it along the top of a ridge about three miles long.

This was the pleasant situation which we were to take over and hold against most determined counter-attacks for the next month. The weather had by now definitely broken and torments of rain fell, turning all the watercourses and streams into raging rivers and the paths and tracks into seas of mud.

Mountainous terrain near Subiaco   List

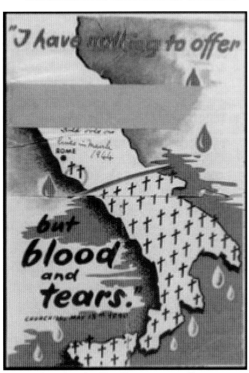

Another leaflet fire over our lines

On Monday, October 2nd, I crossed the pass for Firenzuola for the first time, a fiendish drive in the rain with many traffic blocks. At the end of the day we found ourselves in a very narrow valley among the A Echelons near Moraduccio. There was very little room in which to park clear of the road and what space there was, was deep in mud. We found a place half way up the hill and bedded down for the night, which was not made any more comfortable than it need be by heavy showers of rain and a German bomber which bombed and machine-gunned the area at random. Two days later I moved forward again very slowly along the road, as just beyond the village of Valsalvo the road crossed the river Santerno at a gorge and of course the bridge was blown. The Sappers were building a very fine Bailey over the gap, subsequently decorated with a notice: 'Drive slowly. It's the hell of a drop'. It was; a good seventy feet. The temporary diversion round this obstacle was very steep and bad with one way traffic and it took maybe two hours to do this half mile. When conditions were really bad here, traffic blocks sometimes took six hours to clear. Not far beyond we came to Castel del Rio, a small town with a very wide street and nearby a remarkable hump-backed bridge, believed to be of Roman construction, which had survived the demolition charges. Castel del Rio became a convenient centre for units' echelons, and it was always full of troops. Most unfortunately the censors let through a couple of photographs which were quite unmistakable, thinking no doubt that the battle would be well forward by the time of publication. The line however stabilised for the winter with Castle del Rio still within range of the German guns, and almost exactly a month after the photographs appeared in the Illustrated London News they shelled the place out.

30 – MULES ONLY
3 October 1944

On reaching a board by the roadside headed 'Valmaggiore Trail' I took to a Jeep and we bumped up a very bad track to Valmaggiore, a farm house which had been the Americans Brigade H.Q. Forward from here no vehicles could move, and all supplies went by mule along a very bad track deep in mud. The distance was supposed to be three miles, but it took over three hours to cover it. At the end of this nightmare walk was a typical farm-house and here I spent the next seventeen days. The 2nd Coldstream and 3rd Grenadiers were holding M. Battaglia and the 3rd Welsh Guards protected the supply route which ran back on the top of a ridge to Valmaggiore, each battalion with two companies up, as the conditions were so appalling that the companies had to be relieved every three days. The Coldstream RAP dealt with all casualties from October 3rd to the 9th. There was a constant stream of them, nearly all from shell and mortar fire, as the Germans kept the whole position under continual fire. In particular there was a horrible gun, which we called Bologna Bill, firing the most enormous shells at the top of the ridge. Desmond Fortescue with No. 2 Company were up on top, with Bob Palmer and No 4 supporting their right rear, the Grenadiers being on the left. I went up to the Companies with Billy Steele, who was in temporary command, and a very bad walk it was in pouring rain.

The men were very miserable crouching in slit trenches full of water. Every now and then the big gun fired and a thing like an express train came over. Desmond would shout into the telephone: 'My God, there's something coming', and Bob Palmer, listening in half way down the line, would rock with laughter. When Desmond was relieved eventually, he just stood on the floor of the RAP with a beaming face saying over and over again: 'George, I can't tell you how glad I am to get out of that place'. As usual the R.A.P. got all the 'overs' from the hill in front, and it was not possible to get out and about, except when rain reduced the visibility to a hundred yards or so, as there were German snipers all round. Alexis Cassavetti got a bullet through the front of his battle dress quite close to the R.A.P. All supplies etc came up by night.

During the first week the weather was so bad that the Germans could not attack, and we had to endure the shelling and the wet alone. But after the Welsh Guards R.A.P. had relieved the Coldstream on October 9th things started to happen. That night the Grenadier H.Q., which was in a house a hundred yards away down the hill, had a bad stonking which killed and wounded a lot of people. Douglas Berry and Tom Streatfeild-Moore were wounded, the former dying on the way back. A German patrol then surrounded the house, shot the sentries and lobbed grenades into all the windows, killing or wounding everyone except John Nelson. They also shot a sergeant who was leading a mule up to the house, and they must have been very pleased with their patrol, for they bound his wounds up and left him in a blanket on the ground, where we found him next morning quite cheerful and with the Kraut dressing on his wound. All this kept Dai Morris and his RAP very busy during the night and next day. I helped by doing all the documentation and controlling the RAMC stretcher-bearers so that the worst cases got attention first. Colonel John Nelson moved his H.Q. into a barn of our farm, and next night the Germans made a most determined Battalion attack with the RAP as their final objective. At one time, about 3 a.m., they actually got into the farm yard, but were seen off by a Welsh Guards stretcher-bearer corporal firing a Bren gun from the hip. The Germans withdrew and one officer with seventy five men took refuge in a small house not far away. They stuck a white flag through the chimney and surrendered to us during the day.

This was the last serious attack and next day, October 15th, the Grenadiers R.A.P. took over the Welsh. While the Welsh Guards were there the R.A.P. had a direct hit which killed two, including Dai's servant Gdn Sparks, and wounded three RAMC men. Oliver Roome, the squadron-leader of the Sappers, also blew himself up on one of his own Bee-hives, which shook him.

During the next few days we were able to collect and bury some of the dead. The Coldstream took over all the forward positions on the 15th and the Welsh relieved them on the 18th. There was not more than the usual shelling and patrol activity, as by now the advances of the 78th Division and the 1st Division along the valleys west and east of Battaglia respectively had removed the threats to our flanks and communications. I finally left the position, which Brigadier Andrew called the Black Hole of Calcutta, on the 21st and went back to billets in the Santerno valley at Moraduccio, very glad to change my clothes at last and to be able to say Mass again. On the way down the hill I met Brig. Andrew Scott with Gen. Murray. Andrew greeted me with: 'Hullo, George! Dressed for Piccadilly, as usual!' I had not had my clothes off for 17 days!

We remained in the valley till November 3rd, during which time I managed to get down to Florence for a chaplains' conference and Fr Clarke (S.C.F. Italy) came up to Valsalvo to see us. The rain was very heavy all the week and the river in big spate. The battalion moves up to Battaglia again on the 3rd, but our supply route had been changed, and we had a long and trying drive over the passes to Borgo San Lorenzo and then up the parallel road to the east, finishing at Palazzuolo, only about four miles as the crow flies from where we started, though we had driven fifty miles to get there. Here we found ourselves very near 8th Indian Division, and I saw Larry Twomey who was now commanding 52 Field Rgt in that formation. I had had enough of the hills for a bit and I stayed at Palazzuolo with Bde H.Q. till the 19th, when we were withdrawn and concentrated at our old billets at Vicchio. But not for long, for after a few days rest and a visit to Florence we were put in again, this time in a place which we occupied on and off for the next three months, Monte della Aquasalata. The advance of the Fifth Army had now definitely come to a stop against a series of obstacles which it was not possible to overcome in winter on account of supply problems. It was a case of so near and yet so far, for from the front line we could see the Lombardy Plain stretching out in front of us and in clear weather the Alps in the background. Only one more attack was made and that was of a local nature. For the rest of the time we were able to organise regular reliefs within the Brigade every five days, and rest areas in the pleasant Chianti district south of Florence.

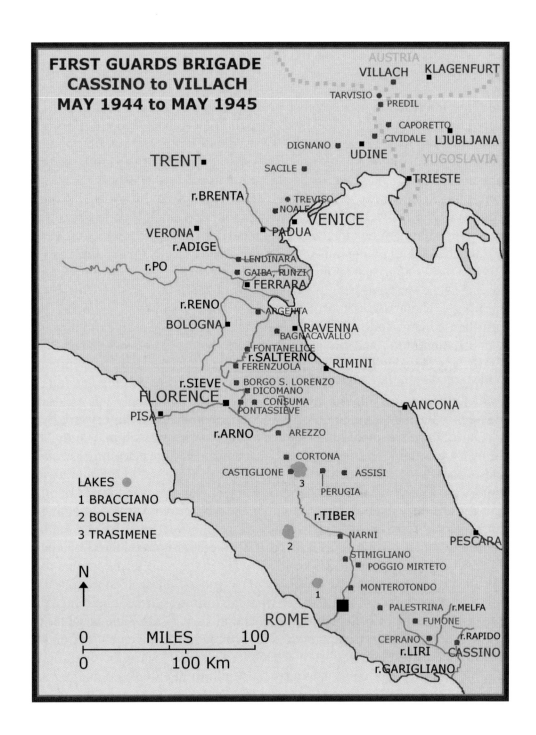

**FIRST GUARDS BRIGADE
CASSINO to VILLACH
MAY 1944 to MAY 1945**

AUSTRIA
VILLACH KLAGENFURT
TARVISIO PREDIL
CAPORETTO
DIGNANO CIVIDALE LJUBLJANA
UDINE YUGOSLAVIA
SACILE

TRENT

r.BRENTA TREVISO
NOALE
VENICE
VERONA PADUA
r.ADIGE TRIESTE
r.PO LENDINARA
GAIBA, RUNZI
FERRARA
r.RENO
ARGENTA
BOLOGNA RAVENNA
BAGNACAVALLO
FONTANELICE
r.SALTERNO
FERENZUOLA RIMINI
r.SIEVE BORGO S. LORENZO
DICOMANO
FLORENCE CONSUMA
PONTASSIEVE
PISA ANCONA

r.ARNO AREZZO

CORTONA
CASTIGLIONE ASSISI
3
PERUGIA

LAKES
1 BRACCIANO r.TIBER
2 BOLSENA NARNI
3 TRASIMENE 2
STIMIGLIANO PESCARA
POGGIO MIRTETO

N
MONTEROTONDO
1
PALESTRINA r.MELFA
FUMONE
ROME CEPRANO r.RAPIDO
0 MILES 100 r.LIRI CASSINO
0 100 Km r.GARIGLIANO

31 – ACQUASALATA & PENSOLA
22 November 1944

Our first duty on Acquasalata began on November 22nd. I went up to S. Appolinare in my truck on the 23rd, a small village about five miles beyond Castel del Rio, where Brigade H.Q. was established in a very poor farmhouse and mule-base in the outhouses. I slept in a stable with Bill Harris, having dined at Bde H.Q. Next day Bill guided me as far as the 'Causeway', a col connecting Monte la Rieve with Monte della Acquasalata. From here the track was in view of the Germans, but they did not mind single figures appearing on it. All walking in the area was a pain and a grief, as the tracks were deep in mud churned up by the mules. I went on alone to Bn H.Q. in a farm called Carre, a most unpleasant spot which could only be approached from directly behind, as the Germans had Spandaus laid on fixed lines past the two ends of the house. There was plentiful evidence of heavy stonking all round, the farm-house being a pile of rubble around and over the one usable room which was battalion H.Q., and the animals outside being very dead indeed. The R.A.P. was a big dug-out in the hillside just below the farm and a crawl-trench led from here into the farm-house. German harassing fire was regular and on a timed programme, and the signal line-men were perpetually out repairing the lines to the companies on the Verro ridge about half a mile forward.

One of the most unpleasing features of the position was sitting waiting for the 4 o'clock afternoon stonk to start. The companies were patrolling as usual, and casualties were steady from that and from shelling and mortaring. It was impossible to visit the forward companies by day except when it was raining heavily, and very inadvisable by night as the whole area was heavily mined. I did go up to Verro one pouring wet day with Colonel Bob Coates and Ashley Ponsonby, and it was not a pleasant trip. We were relieved by the Grenadiers on the 29th by night and had a very bad walk in the mud for two hours to a so-called rest area in reserve. On Friday December 1st I decided to go to the new winter rest area in Chianti to see what the form was there and arrange the Sunday. I found all the Echelons ensconced in very comfortable large farms at Greve and Strada-in-Chianti and fixed up a regular arrangement of Sunday Masses in the area. For the rest of the winter I regularly spent the week up in the line and the week-ends at Strada so as to have the Sundays on a regular organised routine. The contrast between the comfort of Strada and the misery of Acquasalata was too marked; each Monday became harder to bear as the winter passed, and the elation of Friday correspondingly increased.

On Monday December 4th I had a feeling in my bones that something was up, and went back in my truck to Castel del Rio, from where I was lent a Jeep to near the reserve area at Madonna del Rio, to find that the Battalion had moved off five minutes before for the attack on Monte Pensola. I hastened up the track after them as fast as my load of kit would let me and arrived at midnight at Casa Ucellaia where Elston had established the RAP in the upper floor of a farm house. The attack had already started, and when it was at its height Elston's presence was loudly demanded in the stable below, where the farmer and his family occupied one stall, - to deliver a calf! Casualties soon began to come in, and we dealt with about thirty, mostly from S Company, including John Inskip, who had had his eye shot out by a German officer, and C.S.M. Young with both eyes damaged, his right hand blown off and both legs broken, also multiple wounds all up his body – all from one grenade. He lived, but both legs had to come off later. Later in the morning a young Scots Guards corporal came in with two Spandau bullets through the back of his head. Curious to relate both he and John Inskip were walking cases. We heard also that John Lumley was lying out wounded in front, and a party went with a Red Cross flag to fetch him. He had a broken leg and was cheerful, but looked awfully grey, and died two days afterwards.

The attack was completely successful, and two days later the Germans pulled back, leaving us in complete possession of Monte Pensola, which they had regarded as inaccessible from our side. How the Scots Guards ever got up the almost perpendicular slope is a mystery. Bob Coates and Richard Coke got D.S.O.s for this battle, which was the last attack that we made before the reorganization in March.

The Battalion was relieved by the Welsh Guards on the night of the 9th, and we had an execrable walk down to near Madonna del Rio. The liquid mud was above our knees for a lot of the way and as the night advanced it started to freeze. When at last we staggered into our billets I thought my legs and feet would never be warm again and sleep was almost impossible. We were all about 'all-in', and the men's billet was very unsuitable, a church like an ice-house. Next day was Sunday, and everyone slept and cleaned up as well as they could. On Monday, my truck having gone back already, I hitch-hiked back to Strada, getting seven lifts and taking eight hours. The battalion followed during the night and we had our first spell at Strada during the week

32 – FONTANELICE, CITY OF THE DEAD
December 1944

I went into Florence a couple of times, and on finding that the Battalion would be in the line again for Christmas I decided to spend it with them and made other arrangements for the Strada-Greve area. I went up forward again on December 21st, hitch-hiking from Scarperia. On reaching Castel del Rio I found that the area had been reorganised. Brigade H.Q. and the ADS had established themselves in Fontanelice, a rather pleasant little town on the main road to Imola and the terminus of a branch line railway from there. The Germans were holding the Vena del Gesso, a chalk cliff which ran across the valleys in these parts and was sheer on our side. A village called Borgo Tossignano two miles down the main road was occupied by Italian partisans, and was really in No-Man's Land. The Rifle Brigade were on the right of the road facing Tossignano, a village on a precipitous hill which they attacked and were driven out of again. The Brigade front was now stabilised with two battalions forward, the right hand one on Monte Pensola and the left on Monte della Acquasalata.

I got a lift from a military policeman in a Jeep for the last five miles into Fontanelice, a piece of road which always gave me the creeps, as you never knew when it would be stonked. There were a lot of civilians about, and they must have been in touch with the Germans, as a heavy stonk invariably started whenever a relief was taking place. Eventually we cleared the area of civilians, but the road was still harassed, and I was always delighted if the vehicle which answered my 'thumb' was a Dingo! My policeman landed me at Fontanelice at the same time as a heavy stonk. I leaped for the nearest ditch and lay there till they stopped, as it was hard to tell in the dark and among the houses exactly where the shells were landing. At length I got up and walked round the corner where I met Bryce Knox (Battery Commander, Ayrshire Yeomanry) who had been standing in a doorway talking to a Grenadier sergeant when a shell came down which killed the sergeant and demolished a jeep standing nearby. Bryce was only scratched: 'The Knox luck again', he said. He had been slightly wounded three times and had a Military Cross and two bars. He showed me where Brigade Headquarters was, in a large and comfortable house which luckily was not marked on the map and so was not registered by the German guns, though the trees of the avenue had been much damaged by shell-fire. I billeted myself on the Grenadiers for the night in the town, which was like a city of the dead and very heavily damaged.

On the 22nd I went with Humphrey Fitzroy up to the battalion at Carre. The route was new to me, and entailed first crossing the Santerno by a ferry boat pulled over on a guide rope. At the site of the bridge there was also a cable ropeway used for ferrying stores and stretchers with casualties. From the left bank there was a Jeep track up to the sub-A.D.S. at Casa Tombarella and we went up in an ambulance Jeep, a very steep and narrow track only just passable by Jeep. This was the only time I went up it by Jeep, I am glad to say, for though it had been swept there were still box mines about and a loaded Jeep with two casualties on it set one off and was blown to bits a few days later, and of the four men in it there was nothing left to bury. From Tombarella we had the usual muddy scramble up to the Causeway and on to Carre, arriving in good time for the daily 4 o'clock stonk. Next day it snowed hard, which made the conditions much easier for moving about, as one could walk on top of the snow after it froze. Though it was colder, we were really better off than in the mud and we had plenty of warm clothing of American wind-proof material and also white camouflage suits to wear over everything else.

33 – CHRISTMAS MASS IN A DUGOUT
25 December 1944

My first care was to find a place for Christmas Mass and I was lucky enough to find a dugout where only one man slept and he lent it to me. There was just room for three to kneel upright and I put up an ammunition box for an altar and vested and did everything on my knees. With Michael and Reggie in attendance I said the first two Christmas Masses in this way and, for the third, walked back to Monte la Pieve where Ian Fraser collected about seven of S Company and I used the manger in the stable, appropriately, for an altar. Christmas Day was on a Monday, and next day I walked down to Brigade H.Q. in two hours and a half and after lunch there returned to Strada in a T.C.V., the Grenadiers having been relieved during the night, a journey which took another six hours, and very cold it was going over the pass. At Strada I found – oh, joy! – that a proper bath was available with water heated by a wood-fired geyser, my second since January 27th at Constantine, as I did have one in Rome in August; this was one more thing to look forward to when coming out of the line.

After attending H.Q. Coy's Christmas dinner on the 29th and doing the Sunday in the area I returned to Carre on New Year's Day, being very lucky with hitch-hikes and completing the journey in seven and a half hours. Next night the Germans seem to have thought we were going to do an attack, so they put down on the battalion area in D.F. over a thousand shells and about sixty rockets, resulting in two men being slightly wounded. These rockets had been puzzling the authorities and they sent up an expert from A.F.H.Q. at Caserta to vet them. He arrived at Brigade dressed in service dress and brown shoes, and Brigadier Andrew sent him up the hill straight away, where he arrived just in time to get a front seat for this party. When he returned to Brigade next morning he expressed himself as most interested in front line conditions and said they had no idea at Caserta what it was like in the line in wintertime. 'Well, I hope you will tell them when you get back' said Brigadier Andrew. 'Sir, I shall do nothing of the kind,' he replied, 'for I just would not be believed!'.

34 – POLISH INTERLUDE
January 1945

Another story of this time illustrates the toughness of the Germans and those whom they had forced into their army. We had been told to get a prisoner and we shot up a German patrol and picked up one of them with a fractured femur. After splinting him up we sent him down the hill, the stretcher being strapped to a toboggan and pulled along by the stretcher party. In this way and by Jeep he reached the river, but the cable-way was out of order, so he was put in the boat and ferried over by a Grenadier Corporal. The river was in spate with snow-water and half way over the boat sank, throwing them into the water. The corporal, a strong swimmer, just made the bank, and the party meeting them from the ADS thought that the Kraut had had it. They searched along the bank and heard a cry of: 'Englander, Englander', and there he was, hanging on to some bushes. They pulled him out and carried him up the last quarter of a mile to the ADS, where Nigel Nicolson, the Bde I.O. was waiting to interrogate him. It was now 2 a.m. and Nigel thought he would hardly be able to say anything. However he asked for an officer and said: 'Before I go from here I want to tell you all I can about my company. I hate and detest them and hope you will kill the lot.' He was a Pole who had been forced into the German Army and he further said that there were many more who would come over, but the Germans N.C.O.s saw to it that they had no chance.

On Friday January 5th we were relieved by the Welsh Guards and I hitch hiked back to Strada. Next time they went up, on the 10th, I let myself off as I was a bit worse for wear. Outside Carre there was one latrine, field pattern, single seated, heavily encased in sandbags and open to the sky. It was not easy to get in there as there was nearly always some Guardsman or other inside, and it was not a healthy occupation waiting outside the sandbags. During this tour in the line I had a slight go of dysentery, and had to go out to the latrine at four in the morning, thinking that at all events I would be left in peace. It was a very dark night, and a patrol mistook the track and walked right through the latrine. As each man stepped over my feet he said: 'Good morning, Sir!' I could not think up a suitable reply.

Elston at this time was seized with a passion for excavation and improvement and he improved our dug-out so vigorously that it fell in and had to be re-made in a different place, Dai Morris and the Welsh Guards not being at all amused. As a result I found on my next visit, after a blessed fortnight in Strada, that there was no room for me at Carre, and I accordingly made my headquarters at the ADS at Fontanelice with Toffee Field and walked up to the battalion positions each day, getting back each night for dinner at Brigade. In this way I saw a lot of people and got a lot of exercise. I nearly always finished after dark, and it was a weird experience watching the light go and then hearing in the stillness of the night the purring of the German Spandaus, so much more rapid-firing than our Brens, and sounding so much closer than they really were.

35 – A REGULAR WINTER ROUTINE
February 1945

For the next three weeks this was my regular routine, forward on the Monday to Fontanelice and back to Strada on the Friday for the week-end. Nothing much occurred during this time, except that Colonel Blewitt took over command of the 1st Field Ambulance from Toffee, and for a time Colonel Douglas Darling of the 7th R.B. commanded the Brigade in the absence of Brigadier Andrew on leave. I came down the hill for the last time on Friday February 9th. In the middle of February the Brigade was relieved, the Welsh Guards having a most unfortunate experience on their last day, when a salvo of mortar bombs landed on a company just as they queued up for breakfast in a place which was supposed to be quite safe, and they lost several good men.

We moved to Spoleto in Umbria on the 22nd, after one or two farewell parties in Florence, where Fr Vincent Cavanagh was now area chaplain, and a farewell parade for 'S' Company Scots Guards, who had had a most distinguished fighting record with the 2nd Coldstream since Cassino. Their honours included two D.S.O.s, one M.C., two D.C.M.s and nine M.M.s, which must almost be a record for one company.

At Spoleto were also 24th Guards Brigade, and this was to be the end of my happy association with the 2nd Coldstream, as the two Brigades were to reorganise with the 3rd Grenadiers and 3rd Welsh Guards in 1st Guards Bde and the 2nd Coldstream and 1st Scots Guards in 24th Gds Bde. All the rest were to go home, and that meant nearly all of those who had been out longest and the loss of many old friends. I had little to do at Spoleto, so went on leave to Rome for four days, staying at Maryknoll with Fr Dietz of the American Missionaries, which was much more comfortable than last time. I also went one day to Norcia from Spoleto, as it is the birth-place of St Benedict, but was rather disappointed with it. Father 'Dolly' Brookes came up from Caserta to see me at Spoleto and to sort out matters with the rather difficult chaplain of 24th Gds Bde. It was decided that I was to stay on with 1st Gds Bde, now commanded by Gerald Verney, and live at Brigade Headquarters. On Sunday March 11th the party for England left Spoleto and were finished with the war.

We had a final lunch at the transit hotel and I have never been at a more gloomy party. The reconstituted 2nd Coldstream had already gone off to the Ravenna area, and on March 13th we took the road for Fermo, on the Adriatic. I travelled independently , having acquired a new truck in the exchanges, and called at Assisi on the way to see Reggie Secondé who had broken his leg badly in a Jeep accident. David Cazenove and Raymond Firth were also in No. 5 General Hospital at Assisi. I arrived at Fermo in the evening to find I had been allotted a very comfortable billet in a house with a Dutch lady who had once been a Prima Donna. The whole Brigade, now made up by the addition of the 1st Welch Regiment, were in Fermo and Porto San Giorgio, four miles apart, and a lot more of 6th Armoured Division as well, so it was possible to get a lot done in preparation for the final battles.

It was also the second half of Lent and we got a great many Easter duties done, and had the privilege of Holy Week, not only out of battle, but in an Archiepiscopal city as well. Brigade Headquarters was in a villa owned by Contessa Vinci right opposite the Cathedral and I attended all the services there. Also one day I took the Brigadier to pay an official call on the Archbishop, which he returned. We spent exactly four weeks in this delightful area, which was almost untouched by the war, and then on April 10th we were called forward to Cesena to await the result of the final attempt to break the German line in the Argenta gap.

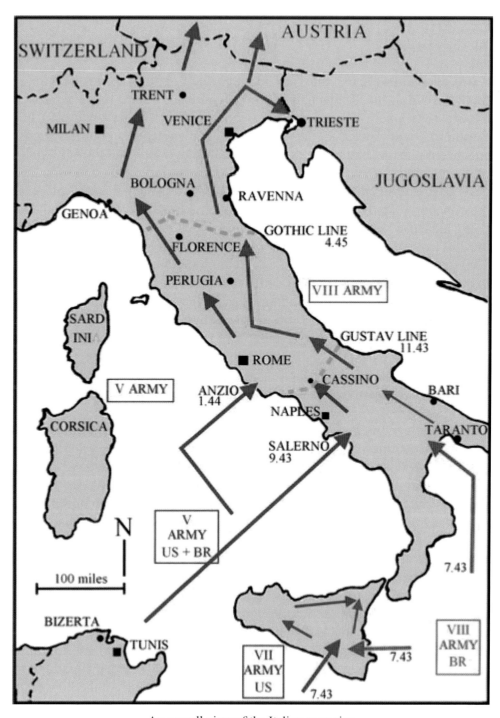

An overall view of the Italian campaign

36 – THE ARGENTA GAP
10 April 1945

It was a long day's drive, of over 100 miles, via Loreto, Ancona and Rimini, finally crossing the Rubicon, a puny little stream, before passing through Cesena to a small village lying between the Via Emilia (Route 9) and Bertinoro. I was billeted on the parish priest in a wretchedly poor little house attached to the tiny church. In the course of the day we passed the battlefields of the previous September round Rimini, where the devastation showed how desperate had been the fighting. We were to be nearly a week in this place, as 6th Armoured Division was the last reserve of Eighth Army and was only going to be used for the final break-through. I took the opportunity of visiting the 2nd Coldstream in the woods north of Ravenna near the Comacchio spit. They were now in 56 Div. And did not care much for it, nor for their return to a purely infantry role, with aquatic adventures in Fantails on the Lago di Comacchio in prospect. Bob Southey was in very poor shape, as he and the doctor had returned from a party the night before, taken the ramp of a Bailey bridge too fast and landed on the other side upside down. On the way back I dined at Eighth Army H.Q. in Cesena with Bunty Scrope and Tim Ahern, who entertained me first in one of their magnificent caravans towed by a 3-tonner. 'Of course, it's only plywood' said Bunty apologetically; but that is the way to go to war!

The battle seemed to be going well, for we were moved on April 16th to a new concentration area near Bagnacavallo, between Ravenna and Faenza, ready to break out through whichever gap opened, to Ferrara and the Po or to Bologna and Milan. Two days later the die was cast, and we moved to Argenta on the Ferrara road. Being with Brigade H.Q. I did not see much of the battle, particularly as the country was quite flat. The Welsh Guards made good the line of the Morte di Primaro and the Welch Regiment passed through them to take the line of the Fossa Combalina, which the enemy were expected to defend strongly. They got across, but were pushed back again with about thirty casualties. The 17/21st Lancers got across the Combalina two miles further south [*vere* west.], and got into Poggio Renatico, and to support this thrust the Welch Regiment attacked again and the Grenadiers passed through them to take S. Bartolomeo, which they did fairly easily. On the 22nd the Armoured Brigade exploited their success, the 2nd Lothian and Border Horse taking Bondeno, and the Derbyshire Yeomanry reaching the banks of the Po west of Ferrara on the morning of St George's Day, the 23rd.

The country was peculiarly unsuited to swanning about on foot, as there were a lot of mines about and the battle was in a fluid state, so I stuck to my truck and moved with Brigade H.Q. to Madonna dei Boschi. The last German shells that I saw fell about two hundred yards away from us.

The Grenadiers were chosen to make the assault crossing of the Po at midnight on the 24th April, and a big concentration of amphibious vehicles was made at Palantone, screened from German eyes by the enormous southern levee of the river. The crossing was made at the site of a German ferry, and was a tremendous success, as the Germans were just carrying out a relief with troops newly arrived from Venezia Giulia who had not seen the ground, and so there was practically no opposition. The New Zealanders crossed on our left and also managed to get a pontoon bridge across. I got over by this bridge on the 26th and we moved to Runzi, where we spent a very wet night. We were now pressing on to the Adige, and moved again next morning to Rasa, a little village west of Lendinara. I was suffering from a Whitlow on my thumb, and Dai Morris insisted on sending me back to the F.D.S. at Gaiba on the north bank of the Po, where they operated on it under a general anaesthetic. However I managed to escape and rejoin the Brigade next afternoon, H.Q. being still at Rasa, but moving in the afternoon to Cavazzana on the other side of Lendinara. We were now across the Adige and from here began our third big advance of the war, and the most thrilling of the three, which only ended on the other side of the Alps.

37 – ACROSS THE ALPS
30 April 1945

The German resistance was completely broken, and apart from an attempt to get their best troops, the 1st and 4th Parachute Divisions, back into the Austrian redoubt round Berchtesgaden by the Brenner Pass, which failed because the Italian partisans and Americans got there first, they surrendered to us more or less where they stood. It became a question, then, of a race to get to Austria and Trieste before the Jugo-Slavs, and since the Armoured Brigade could not get their tanks over the Po (they never did succeed in doing this), the two lorried infantry brigades of 6th Armoured division were directed on Austria with all speed. Starting from Cavazzana on Monday April 30th we moved very slowly along congested roads through Padua to Noale. The New Zealanders had entered Venice the day before, and were making for Trieste.

We crossed the Piave at Treviso on May 1st and stayed at Sacile that night. Next day we reached the Tagliamento and found that the river had risen in the night and the concrete ford built by the Germans just above the blown bridge was impassable. This caused some delay and eventually we found an unblown bridge about five miles upstream at Dignano and pushed on to reach Udine in the afternoon. Here we first met Tito's troops, who had made a bad second into the city, but were claiming it for Tito. Their general policy was to grab as much of Venezia Giulia as they possibly could, and they caused us acute anxiety in all our dealings with them for the next few weeks. This day, May 2nd, was the day on which the Germans in Italy surrendered to Field Marshal Alexander, but neither we nor they knew about it till later. Also some of the troops between us and the Austrian frontier refused to recognise the validity of the surrender, as they were not under command of von Vietinghoff, but of von Loehr, C-inC. South East.

But the greatest difficulty was our 'allies' the Jugo-Slavs. The Welsh Guards had to go to Cormona, south of Udine, to separate a force of Chetniks, who were fighting their own battle with the Jugs, and disarm and intern them. The Grenadiers went to Cividale, ten miles east of Udine, to keep the peace between Italian partisans and Jugs, and the Welsh regiment were sent beyond them to Caporetto, where they found the Jugs in full possession. The Germans north of Udine were most unwilling to let us come forward and we made a hurried concentration of all the artillery we could raise and threatened to blast them out of it. They then withdrew, blowing the bridges as they went, and on May 7th von Loehr consented to allow us to enter Austria unopposed.

The 8th of May, V.E. Day, saw the last scene of all. We moved very early in the morning via Cividale, Caporetto and the Predil Pass, seeing many monuments of the 1914-18 war on the way, and crossed the frontier into Austria near Tarvisio before midday. It was a marvellous mountain country, quite unspoilt by the war, but our chief feeling was one of relief that we had not been obliged to fight through the Alps. We arrived at Villach in the afternoon, to find an incredible situation, Austrians greeting us with intense joy as liberators, British ex P.O.W. in great quantities (all other ranks, no officers except one Coldstream, Andrew Mayes, who was in hospital), and many thousands of displaced persons of almost every possible nationality, even Chinese. We hoisted the Union Jack ceremoniously in the evening and listened to Churchill's broadcast on the end of the war. But there was no time to rest, hardly even to think.

We had several acute problems to solve, and Brigadier Gerald made me responsible for all ex-British P.O.W.s in the area. There were about 400 of these based on a camp in Villach and boarded out on farms round about, mostly prisoners from Crete and Tobruk who had been behind wire for four years, including Australians and New Zealanders. An excellent man, Sgt Bowman of the Warwicks Yeomanry, who had been a 'man of confidence' in the camp, had all the organization under control and was the greatest help to me. Most of them, of course, of course, wanted to go home at once, but some had made friends with the Austrians and wanted a month's leave in the country. It was useless ordering them about, especially the Australians, but by tact and good humour we got them all evacuated by air on May 11th. Sergeant Bowman volunteered to remain behind to help the French P.O.W. Unfortunately he got shot in the chest by someone carelessly handling a Luger pistol, and had to go to hospital. We put him in for the B.E.M. but I never heard whether he got it or not.

We were moved again on the 12th to deal with another problem, the Jugoslav frontier. This ran along the tops of high and impassable mountains south of the River Drava, but the Jugs would not remain behind it and were trying to occupy the whole of Carinthia. The Austrians were terrified of Jug occupation and implored us to protect them. Eventually after much diplomatic pressure they withdrew to the frontier, though they remained in Istria, and the Brigade was deployed south of the Worthersee to see that they did not come down again. There were only two real routes to JugoSlavia, the railway tunnel and the road over the Loibl Pass.

Brigade headquarters was in a delightful chalet-inn on the Keutschacher see which was known as the Grenadiers' Arms. The Grenadiers were on the road to the Loibl Pass, the Welsh Guards at Rosegg opposite the tunnel, and the Welsh Regiment strung out in between along the south bank of the River Drava. There we remained till the end of June, when orders came to return to Italy en route for England. On May 27th we had a Divisional Mass of Thanksgiving at Klagenfurt Cathedral. I sang the Mass, at which there were about 500 Catholics present, which was very good considering our commitments.

On June 29th there was a farewell parade of 1st Guards Brigade at Viktring and the move to Fano on the Adriatic near Ancona began next day, Brigade Headquarters and the 3rd Grenadiers and 3rd Welsh Guards only being concerned.

I travelled independently, and was surprised to find snow lying at the roadside on the pass to Tarvisio. We went by Pontebba and Udine, avoiding Gorizia, as the Jug situation there was obscure, and reaching Trieste in the evening where we stayed with the 2nd Coldstream in very uncomfortable, almost active-service, conditions in the hills outside the town. It seems to be a very poor country, the hinter-land of Trieste, very different from the lovely pine-forests and lakes of Carinthia, and I should say Tito was welcome to it. All the villages had painted out their Italian names and substituted Jugoslav ones consisting apparently entirely of consonants.

38 – WEEK-END IN VENICE
July 1945

Next day I went on to Venice and spent a delightful week-end at the Horlicks' villa, the Giardenia Eden, on the Giudecca, which the Coldstream had the use of for an officers' leave centre. On Monday July 2nd we went on to Fano, by way of Padua, Ferrara and Forli. Here we were attached to the I.R.T.D. in the very badly damaged town, and I had a room in a large and gloomy house. Brigade H.Q. kept their mess together in a small villa, and the battalions were under canvas. There was absolutely nothing to do and it was terribly hot. The authorities knew nothing about our move home and left us there to rot for a month.

I luckily still had my truck and in the second week went off to Rome for four days, staying with the kind Fr Dietz again at Maryknoll. I visited S. Anselmo and talked to the Abbot Primate. It was unpleasantly hot in Rome and I returned to Fano, a seven hours run, on July 12th. I also went to Ancona several times, where Fr Nicholas Holman was in charge of the area, and went one day to see the Republic of San Marino, and another to Loreto. Meanwhile the men were getting bored and impatient, and Cpl. Chriscoli in the Grenadiers slugged a military policeman and was court-martialled. He had got a good M.M. in Italy and was eventually killed in Malaya in 1949.

At last the War Office began to enquire why we were not back, as we were next wanted to go into 3rd Division, train and be equipped in Kentucky, and take part in 'D' Day on the mainland of Japan! Things began to move in the fourth week of July, and we handed in all our trucks &c, as we were to be flown home. We left Fano in a train of box cars on Sunday July 29th and, after 22 hours in the train, arrived at Foggia in S. Italy! Twenty four hours later, after reveille at 2 a.m. we were taken to an aerodrome, from which we took off in Liberators at 7 a.m. and flew to England. Most of the way we were above the clouds at 9000 feet, and I was lucky in getting a seat by a window from which I got glimpses of Rome, the tip of Corsica, Marseilles and the Channel. We crossed the English coast near Brighton and flew over Reading, then turned north-east and landed at Glatton, an aerodrome at Conington south of Peterborough, at 3 o'clock; such is modern travel.

After passing the customs and doctors we went to a very pleasant transit camp and I went for a walk, finding myself at Holme station, watching the north expresses from Kings Cross go through, a welcome sight after two and a half years abroad.

Next day, by way of contrast, they took us to Peterborough in T.C.V.s and by train from there to Hawick, which took much longer than from Italy to England, and we did not get to Stobs camp till midnight. The 1st Irish Guards and 201 Guards Bde, now commanded by Brigadier Hugh Norman, made us very welcome, fitted us out with medal ribbons, and sent us on disembarkation leave. There was a heat-wave in Scotland at the time, but though we were in battle-dress we hardly noticed it. I was on leave from August 4th to 27th, and during that time the war with Japan ended, so on my return to Stobs I found we were not going to Kentucky, but to Palestine instead.

39 – PALESTINE, VICTORY CAMP & RELEASE
September-October 1945

A great many changes in 1st Guards Brigade were pending when I returned from leave. Brigade Headquarters was re-forming at Bowhill, a house belonging to the Duke of Buccleuch near Selkirk, under Eddie Goulburn as Brigadier in place of General Verney, who had not returned with us from Austria. Michael Howard succeeded John Buchanan as Brigadier Major and all the other officers had been changed as well. The 3rd Grenadiers were at Wilton Camp, Hawick, and were being completely reorganized under Colonel Peter Clifton, but the 3rd Welsh Guards in Selkirk were to be disbanded. The other two battalions of the Brigade, the 3rd Coldstream (Colonel Bob Coates) and the 1st Welsh Guards (Colonel Reggie Hodgkinson), were not even in Scotland, but at Kington in Herefordshire. While the reshuffle took place there was nothing for me to do except say a Sunday Mass at Bowhill, so I made the most of the week-time and divided the time between Rothiemay and Ampleforth, finally returning to Bowhill on Thursday October 4th.

We moved very early on the 6th by stopping trains to Liverpool where we boarded the Holland Amerika liner *Volendam* at the Landing Stage. During the night the 3rd Coldstream and 1st Welsh arrived from Herefordshire and embarked. There were also other drafts and quite a number of civilians, who were full of complaints about their accommodation. We sailed at 10.30 a.m. next day and it was extremely pleasant to meet again many friends of the old

1st Guards Brigade and the Guards Armoured Division. I was in a cabin with four Welsh Guards officers. In peace time it would have been two-berth, now it had six berths in tiers and five of us in it, so there was not much room. But I thoroughly enjoyed the voyage, which was calm all the time.

We did not touch anywhere between Liverpool and Haifa, passed Gibraltar early on the fourth day out, and skirted the north coast of Africa seeing such familiar places as Algiers, Philippville, Carthage, Cape Bon and Pantelleria. We sailed all along the south coast of Crete and after that the next land we saw was Mount Carmel at dawn on the 17th, the eleventh day out from Liverpool. We landed at 8.30 a.m. at Haifa, which is a very fine modern harbour built entirely during the British mandate, and even a big ship like the *Volendam* (17,000 tons) could tie up at the quay-side. It was very warm, especially as we were in battle-dress, and we were quickly loaded into 3-tonners and driven off to a big camp at Pardess Hanna in the plain of Sharon

Back in his Community:
Paul Nevill, George Forbes, Stephen MarwoodAmpleforth 194

about 25 miles south of Haifa.

Political tension at this time was not high, as the United Nations Commission was sitting in Jerusalem and neither Jews nor Arabs wanted to jeopardise their case by violence, though this did not restrict the activities of the Stern gang. We had come to the country direct from England and entirely free from prejudices, but we were only a very short time in Palestine before our sympathies swung very definitely over to the Arabs and away from the Jews.

The next week or two, during which the Grenadiers arrived in a different ship, were left for us to shake ourselves down and become acclimatized. Also we got out our khaki drill pretty quick. The camp at Pardess Hanna was a very large one, of tents pitched on concrete bases and some permanent huts for messing etc. There was a large concrete cinema and various shops within the barbed-wire perimeter. The camp held the whole Brigade with ease.

Wc had comc out without transport, and drew our allotment, a very sorry lot of vehicles, on the usual army principle of peace-time, that no new vehicle (and there were plenty of them) might be issued for used till the one it replaced literally fell to bits. I never had a truck in Palestine that would go, and most of the Jeeps that I borrowed were in the last stages of decrepitude. I had to fight Divisional Headquarters to get a Jeep allotted to me at all, and that died on me very soon.

40 – PARISH PRIEST OF GALILEE
November 1945

At the end of October we took over security duties which covered the whole of Galilee except for Haifa itself. Brigade Headquarters moved to Safad, a summer resort in the hills between the Sea of Galilee and the frontier, the 3rd Grenadiers to Ez Zib near the frontier-post on the road from Haifa to Tyre, where they occupied a very primitive camp, and the 1st Welsh Guards to Tiberias, where they took over a luxury hotel, with the Prince of Wales Company up at Metulla, the frontier post on the road to Damascus. The Coldstream remained at Pardess Hanna for the meantime, ready to look for illegal immigrants landing on the coast of Caesarea. I remained at Pardess Hanna at first, as Fr Byrne (2nd Infantry Bde) was at Nazareth and covering north Galilee.

On November 24th the peace was rudely shattered by a big bang in the night. The Jews, probably Stern gang, had blown up the Police Station on the coast near Hadera to cover the landing of some illegal immigrants in small boats. The battalion was called out to cordon the area and search the Jewish settlements. On the 26th there was a conference of chaplains at Latroun which Fr McCreton, the S.C.F. Middle east, had called. I went there by inland road, Ein Shemer-Tulkanu-Qalqiliya, through Arab country, and my truck was loudly cheered by the Arabs! The Cistercian monastery (destroyed, alas, in the fighting later) at Latroun was a marvellous place, a most fertile oasis in the barren foothills between Jaffa and Jerusalem. Fr Rudesind Brookes, now S.C.F. Palestine on transfer from Athens, was there. After the conference I went down to see Philip Barry who was in 6th Airborne Division at Qastina. It was a long drive back, but the road are excellent tarmac, all British made.

1st Division, less 1st Guards Brigade, were now being withdrawn to the Delta to refit, and they were temporarily relieved by 3rd Division from the Canal Zone. To my great surprise I found the old 33rd Field Regiment R.A. driving in to Pardess Hanna camp, whom I had not seen since I left them at Milborne Port in 1941. Of course they were much changed, the only officer remaining being Brown the Quartermaster, but I also found Tony Kevill, now a Major, and still with 20th A/T Regiment.

By mid December the moves were complete and I was able to hand over the Pardess Hanna area to one of the 3rd Division chaplains. I arranged to spend Christmas at Tiberias with 1st Welsh Guards. Of course I would have liked to go to Bethlehem, but this was impossible as I had Masses at Tiberias and Rosh Pinna. At the end of the year there were further moves, Brigade Headquarters moving to Nazareth and the Coldstream to Megiddo camp in the Plain of Jezreel. I moved to Nazareth myself on December 31st.

For the next month I was privileged to be the parish priest of the (military) parish of Galilee. From headquarters in the Austrian hospice in Nazareth kept by the Brothers of St John of God, where I had the use of the chapel, I travelled daily over the roads which our Blessed Lord must have known so well, to Cana of Galilee, Tiberias, Capharnaum, the Mount of the Beatitudes, Tabigha (Bethsaida), Naim etc., with occasional visits to No 42 General Hospital at Haifa to see Ralph Gilbey or Danny Dixon who had been injured in road accidents, and up to Divisional Headquarters in the Carmelite monastery on Mount Carmel. One day I went down to the big cantonment at Sarafand to see Martin Howard, on another we took a convoy of Jeeps up to the top of Mount Tabor, and occasionally I took parties round the sights of Nazareth.

It was a peaceful and happy time, culminating with a retreat for all M.E.F. chaplains in the Italian hospice on the Mount of Beatitudes during the first week of February. It was given by Fr Lamb, a 90-year old Carmelite from Mount Carmel who still acted as officiating chaplain to the troops in Haifa. A lot of chaplains came up from Egypt and they brought me a posting order for home, so I was to leave 1st Guards Brigade after being with them for just on three years in North Africa, Italy, Austria and Palestine, almost a record for a chaplain's appointment.

Michael Howard had been posted to the Staff College and left for England on the 9th, and on the 11th I despatched my heavy baggage from Haifa, had a farewell lunch with the Coldstream, and went to Jerusalem for three days leave, as I was quite determined not to go home without seeing the Holy Places. Fr Rudesind had arranged for me to stay at the Dormition Abbey, and he also got an officer who had been there a long time to show me round. We wasted no time and I was able to see all the sights of Jerusalem and Bethlehem, an unforgettable experience. On the 14th Fr Rudesind came with us to Emmaus. I did not have time to go down to Jericho and the Dead Sea.

On the 15th I returned to Nazareth by way of Nablus (Samaria), said good-bye to Brigade and caught the Cairo mail at Haifa. I had sleeping berth and was turned out of it at Kantara East at 3.30 a.m., to wait five hours, cross the Canal and entrain for Port Said. The Port Said train was crowded and I had to stand, but it was only an hour's run. A truck took me to 156 Transit Camp at Port Fouad on the east bank of the Canal. After three days of discomfort and sand-storms we embarked on the 19th in S.S. *Princess Kathleen* a 6000 ton ferry boat belonging to the C.P.R. and normally plying between Vancouver and Victoria B.C. She had three funnels and was fast, but rolled a lot in any sea. We sailed at 4.30p.m. and had a good voyage to Malta, where we refuelled, arriving at 7.30 a.m. on the 22nd and leaving at 2 p.m. the same day. A storm had arisen, so we hugged the east coast of Sicily for shelter and I saw Cape Passero where I landed in 1943.

We passed through the Straits of Messina at midnight and made very heavy weather of the passage to the north tip of Corsica, where we had to take violent avoiding action to escape a loose mine. The weather was so rough we had to slow down and did not dock at Toulon till 8 a.m. on the 25th. This was the first lap of 'Medloc' route, and we were taken to a transit camp at La Crau near Hyeres. We left Toulon station at 10 p.m. on the 26th in a German train which had no heating and travelled by Nimes, Narbonne, Carcassonne, Toulouse, Limoges, round the Ceinture at Paris, and Pontoise to Dieppe, with halts for breakfast and supper on the 27th, and arriving at Dieppe at 10 a.m. on the 28th. Here we went to a rather superior transit camp, and were embarked next day, March 1th, in the *Royal Daffodil*, one of the Margate steamers from London (General Steam Navigation), and, after a very rough crossing, landed at Newhaven at 11 a.m. I heard we were the last boat to cross the Channel for several days. I reported to the War Office, on reaching London at 3 p.m., was sent on leave, and caught the Aberdonian from Kings Cross that night.

41 – AFTERMATH
Summer 1946

After four weeks on leave I was posted to Scottish Command, and on reporting to Fr Dowd at Edinburgh was sent to No 1 Military Port at Cairnryan, near Stranraer, which was as far away from my home in Scotland as it was possible to put me. I was only there for about five weeks and was then posted to London District for duty with the Victory Parade camps in Hyde Park and Regents Park.

On reporting to London District I found the camps were not open yet, so I was sent to Pirbright for a fortnight to let the chaplain there get some leave. I met many friends there, and on moving eventually to Hyde Park discovered that the whole show was being run by 201 Guards Bde under Brigadier Hugh Norman, and that he had arranged for Elston Grey Turner and me to share a tent in his Brigade H.Q. compound. An amazing number of friends I had made during the war were in the camp, and though it was pretty wet I thoroughly enjoyed it, and it was an excellent ending to six years' service, nearly all of it with the Brigade of Guards. I was not in the Victory Parade, which took place on the Saturday before Whitsun, June 8th, and I am rather glad, as now the sight of troops on the march brings such a flood of memories that I am quite overcome. A week later, on June 15th, I travelled up to York and passed through the release centre at Fulford Barracks, my time overseas entitling me to three full months leave.

Towards the end of my release leave, in mid August, I was sent to take charge of St Oswald's, Padgate, Warrington and remained there for a month, returning to Ampleforth just before term started in September. People have often asked me the question: 'Did you not find it very difficult to settle down to the monastic life again?' The answer is easy. It was just like slipping one's hand into a well-worn glove. For one thing, the monastic life was much easier physically than that which we had been living for the past six years. On top of that was a certain wonder at still being alive, an inability to realise why, when so many better men were dead; and a hope that perhaps God had still some work for us to do.

OTC at camp 1935. These boys were about 25 in 1943: many of them were the younger
officers of the Army who did fight 'for King and Country', from Alamein to Lubeck.
They suggest the quality of the OTC and of the men like Fr George who trained them.

Below left, Victor Cubitt about 17 (p.18 +)   *Below right,* Jim Utley, Rome 1929 (p.69)

APPENDIX

PRISONERS
Problems of liberation

Two days before VE Day the 1st Guards Brigade and a brigade of Greenjackets crossed the border of Italy and Austria as the spear-head of the Eighth Army from Tarvisio and took over the area of Villach, near Klagenfurt. After the cease-fire there were quantities of German soldiers, estimated at 300,000, wandering about, uncertain what to do next. Our first task was to shepherd them into camps under their own officers, who seemed singularly unwilling or incapable of acting with authority, and prepare their return to their own countries. Then we turned to our next job, that of dealing with the vast numbers of D.P.s ('Displaced persons') who had been herded by the advancing allies from all points of the compass. These included nationals of many countries, such as the entire Hungarian army, an engine driver from Bulgaria, who demanded his return with his engine to Bulgaria, refugees from Jugoslavia and the Ukraine, even some Chinese.

All these gave rise to problems of different kinds which were quite beyond the scope of soldiering and more of a political or diplomatic nature especially with our 'allies'. The Austrians were obviously delighted that we and not the Russians had liberated them from the Nazis. We were forbidden to fraternise with them or to allow them to display the Austrian Imperial flag until the situation was clear, but many of the inhabitants were Slovenes (in the parish church at Keutschach I was handed a card at the end of Mass with the Leonine prayers in Slovene). They were apprehensive that the 'Titoists' would take over Carinthia, as they obviously intended to do, but more of this will appear when the question of repatriation arose. This was eventually solved in London, when Tito agreed to withdraw to his pre-war frontier at the Loibl pass on condition that all his 'nationals' should be handed over to him. He refused however to withdraw from Istria as he wanted the port of Trieste and the naval base of Pola. In the meantime we were bidden to restrain the enthusiasm of the 'Jugs' by any means short of open rupture, especially to discourage them from helping themselves to abandoned German arms and stores.

After the Germans had been removed from the camp at Viktring it was used for concentrating the Serbo-Croat D.P.s prior to deciding what to do with them. There were about 10,000 of them, some of whom were Chetniks (who had fought for Mikaelovitch against Tito) but most were peasants who had fled before the advancing Communists; there were men, women and children, with their farm animals. It must be remembered that there was a civil war in progress in Jugoslavia which had nothing to with the war against Germany – or with us. For a time Britain had favoured the Mikaelovitch party, but had changed sides and now supported Tito. Under the agreement to withdraw to his old frontier Tito now claimed the return of his nationals to Jugoslavia. The reaction at Viktring was, 'Don't give us back to Tito to be liquidated'. In the event they were loaded onto trains and sent through the tunnel to the other side. The parish priest of the parish which went up to the frontier post at the Loibl pass told us what happened, having had word from the other side. They took them off the trains, separated all the 'intellectuals' (as he called them) and liquidated them, and let the peasants go. Later they accused us of breaking faith, as the ring-leader whom they particularly wanted jumped the train when he saw where it was going. If he did this in the single-line tunnel he was almost certainly killed.

The Russian and the British forces met about 20 miles to the north of Klagenfurt on the river Gurk, where a temporary cease-fire line was set up. At a bridge over the river the Russians set up a post, armed to the teeth with machine guns. On our side was one British private soldier, entirely unarmed. There was no communication of a social nature between the two sides. The handing over of Soviet subjects took place here, many of whom had fought against us with the Germans but some had fought along with the Italian partisans behind the German lines in Italy: see *Winged Dagger* by Roy Farran. My only knowledge of this affair was at second hand. As part of an armoured Division we had a troop-carrying company of R.A.S.C. who were used to transport them. The officer commanding told me that all his drivers were members of the T.G.W.U. (Ernest Bevin's union) and were full of praise for all things Russian till he put them on one of these convoys. When they came back they never mentioned Russia again.

When Italy pulled out of the war many of our P.O.W.s escaped from the then unguarded camps and made their way, aided by the Italian peasantry, to the Adriatic coast from which we evacuated them from behind the German lines, but many were already moved to Austria and were under German guard till we released them. Under the misapprehension that I had nothing to do my Brigadier ordered me to collect all British P.O.W.s in the area and arrange their repatriation. There were about 2,000 of them who had been captured in the desert, Greece or Crete, among them Australians, New Zealanders and South Africans. There were no officers, but some excellent N.C.O.s, especially one R.S.M. from New Zealand. They had been working on farms and had made such friends that some asked for a month's leave first, and there were the usual cases of men whose wives had been killed in air-raids or who had deserted their husbands for other men. These men had been behind wire for up to three years and were not particularly keen to go home.

The R.S.M. asked to stay for another reason. Some of his men had escaped into Jugoslavia and he wanted to find out about them. We made him up to Captain and gave him all facilities from our side but the Jugs were very unwilling to let him in to their country. Eventually they agreed and he found some news of them in a village. Tito's army welcomed them as reinforcements, but when they said they wanted to go home they were given the choice of concurring or being liquidated. The villagers then showed him their graves.

Yet another factor entered this question of P.O.W.s when we crossed the Rhine and advanced into Germany. The Germans moved all the prisoners that they held away from our advancing troops towards the east, possibly with the idea of using them as bargaining counters. These were liberated after being overrun by the Americans and Russians. There was no difficulty here with the Americans, but the Russians held different views. They said, ' Why do you want these men back? We regard our men who are captured as expended.'

Here then was a dilemma for us. If we refused to hand over the Russians that we had in Austria, what would have been the fate of our own prisoners? There is small room for doubt about the answer. It was one of those cases when whatever answer you give you are bound to be wrong. The attempt to 'frame' Mr Macmillan could hardly be fair. If anyone was to blame it could be the makers of the Yalta agreement, and it is hardly likely that they could foresee how events would turn out. Maybe we can only account these events as 'things lamentably done and ill-done'. Perhaps Roosevelt and Churchill were too naive at Yalta in considering that everyone would treat others as they would themselves.

NOTES ON PEOPLE NAMED
About 230 people by name or title.
Page numbers in bold; marked * if more than once on a page

In this list we have tried to give a minimum of background information. We have been largely dependent on the Internet for this. Although many sites say many things, sometimes listing so many people of the same name one can only guess which instance meets the case, others are passed by in silence. Please tell us of errors or omissions. As Fr George taught and trained many of those he met while they were at school at Ampleforth, this is noted.

There are 233 names mentioned, some several times. All are listed here with a brief note where possible. About 100 are provided with a direct link to the note here, with a return link (Text). 27 of these were taught or trained at school by Fr George, O.C. of the Ampleforth O.T.C.

Abbot Primate: The Abbot of St Anselm's international monastery in Rome, primacy of honour among Benedictine Congregations. At this time Fidelis von Stotzingen, monk of Marialaach, Germany, Primate 1913 till death 1947. **P.90**

Adair, Brigadier Allan: Grenadier Guards, Company Commander WW1, GOC Guards Armoured Division WW2. MC (twice); later Maj-General Sir Allan Adair, 6th Baronet, GCVO,CB,DSO,MC &Bar. *Died* 1988. **P.13**

Ahern, Tim: Ampleforth 1926. Retired 1969 as Maj-Gen. CBE QHS, Director of Medical Services, British Army of the Rhine. *Died* 1980. **P.86**

Alderson, Dick: Capt. R.C., Coldstream Guards, *Killed* 10 June 1944 **p.55-7, 62**

Alexander, General: Irish Guards, MC & DSO(1916). GOC Fourteenth Army, Burma (1941), 15th Army Group, N.Africa & Sicily (1942), Supreme Allied Commander Mediterranean (1943) when Eisenhower moved to NW Europe. Later Earl Alexander of Tunis KG PC GCB OM GCMG CSI DSO MC CD PC(Can). *Died* 1969. **P.88**

Angold, Fr Paulinus OSB: Monk of Buckfast, 1922. Chaplain, Egypt, Italy. Later worked at Buckfast in glass and bell-ringing. *Died* 2009 **P.44, 55**

Angus, Andy: Lieutenant A.D., Grenadier Guards, MC. **P.62**

Archbishop of Malta: Dom Maurus Caruana, monk of Fort Augustus, Scotland 1885, Consecrated 1915; KBE 1918. d. 17 Dec 1943. **P.30**

Bankier, Patrick: Lieutenant, Welsh Guards. *Killed* 27 May 1944. **P.58**

Barry, Philip: Ampleforth A40; Lt, Parachute Regiment. **P.11,94**

Baxendale, John: Lieutenant, Auxiliary Military Pioneer Corps, The Loyal Regiment (North Lancashire) MC. **P.17**

Bell, Willie: Lieutenant W.A.O., Welsh Guards; commissioned 1 Oct 1940. **P.45**

Berry, Douglas: Lieutenant the Hon. J.D., Grenadier Guards. *Killed* 10 October 1944. Son of Viscount Kemsley. **P.17,75**

Bevin, Ernest: Trade Union leader from 1922, wartime Minister of Labour, later Foreign Minister 1945-51. *Died* 1951. **P.99**

Birkbeck, Bill: Captain W., Coldstream Guards. **P.41**

Blewitt, Basil: Colonel, R.A.M.C. (Father of Maj.Sir Shane Blewitt, Ampleforth 1953). **P.83**

Block, David: Lt Colonel, R.A., Ayrshire Yeomanry. Received DSO together with his twin brother Lt-Colonel Adam Block R.A. (Glasgow Herald 17 Dec 1946). **P.55**

Bone, Commodore: Prominent Glasgow shipmaster, working for the Anchor Line; also an author. When he died, his ashes were scattered over the site of the Titanic. **P.14**

Bonsor, David Victor: Major, Grenadier Guards, MC. **P.51, 54**

Boultwood, Fr Alban, OSB: Monk of Fort Augustus, Scotland 1929, sent to St Anselm's, Washington DC, 1946 as Prior, elected Abbot 1961; retired 1975. *Died* 25 March 2009 aged 97. **P.67**

Bowman, Sgt: Prisoner in Syria, Sgt Frederick James Bowman. He did get his BEM. **P.89***

Boylan, Paddy: Colonel, 33 Field Regt R.A. **P.13**

Bridgeman, Humphrey: Lieutenant, Scots Guards. *Killed* 28 May 1944, Monte Cassino. **P.60**

Bright, Mgr Humphrey: Archdiocese of Birmingham. Senior RC Chaplain in Italy. Visiting Rome, just liberated, he was appointed to succeed the future Cardinal Griffin as Auxiliary Bishop of Birmingham, 1944. **P.46, 49**

Brodie Knight, Charles: Captain, Welsh Guards. **P.45**

Brookes, Fr Rudesind OSB: monk of Downside 1926, known as 'Dolly'. Army 1915-24, Chaplain (Irish Guards) 1942. MC 1944. Rector of St Edward's, Malta 1956-66, Rome (English Benedictine Procurator) 1966-77. Autobiography, Father Dolly, 1983. *Died* 17 December 1984. Born de Minciaky: his father was Russian. **P.19, 26, 47, 84, 94, 95***

Brown: Quartermaster, 33 Field Regt R.A. cf. Boylan above. **P.94**

Buchanan, John: Brigade Major, 1st Bn Grenadier Guards 1945, MBE. From 1948 schoolmaster (English) at Shaftesbury, then as HM at Oakham tripled size of school. Obituary *Daily Telegraph* 14 Oct 2005. **P.91**

Bussy, Fr Joseph, SJ: Torpedoed on way back southern Africa, he became Chaplain to the Forces (1942-46; 239276). Later transferred to Oregon Jesuit Province. *Died* there in 1986. **P.16**

Byrne, Corporal: *No data yet.* **P.43**

Byrne, Fr Michael: Chaplain. From Archdiocese of Birmingham, later founder Chaplain of HCPT (Handicapped Children's Pilgrim Trust) 1954. **P.93**

Carthage, Archbishop of: Archbishop Charles-Albert Gounot CM, consecrated 1937. *Died* 1953. **P.33**

Cassavetti, Alexis: Captain, Welsh Guards. Later General Manager, BP, at Athens (1955). **P.75**

Cavanagh, Fr Vincent, OSB: Monk of Downside 1933. In landing at Anzio; later in Florence. Bursar of Downside 21 years. *Died* 5 April 1975. **P.44, 56, 83**

Cazenove, David: Lieutenant D.M.deL., Coldstream (Commission May 1941, 186908). **P.84**

Chaplin, Dick: Major R.M., Coldstream Guards. **P.62**

Charteris, Hugo: Lieutenant, Scots Guards, MC; grandson of Earl of Wemyss. Later wrote novels, TV scripts. *Died* 1970. **P.60 66**

Chetwode, David: Major G.D., Coldstream Guards, MBE. Entered Naval College at Dartmouth (his father was an Admiral), then Sandhurst. **P.18, 55**

Chichester, Desmond: Captain, Coldstream Guards, MC. Later, as Major, ADC to General Alexander, also to Alexander as Governor-General of Canada. *Died* 2000. Obituary, *Daily Telegraph* 24 Oct 2000.. **P.52, 60, 63**

Chriscoli, Cpl: John Patrick, Lance-Cpl, 3rd Bn Grenadier Guards (2621950). MM September 1944. *Killed* Malaya 1949. **P.90**

Churchill, Winston: 4th Hussars 1895; Lt-Colonel, Royal Scots Fusiliers, 1915-17. British Prime Minister & national leader 1940-45. *Died* 1965. **P.35, 88, 100**

Clarke, Fr J.M: Senior Chaplain, from Archdiocese of Westminster: later Apostolic Administrator, Forces Chaplains (equivalent to later Bishop of the Forces). **P.16, 30, 76**

Clifton, Colonel Peter: Lt-Col, Grenadiers, Coldstream, Guards DSO, won at the crossing of the River Po, 24 April 1945. **P.91**

Clive, Bob: *see* Windsor-Clive.

Coates, Colonel Bob: later Milnes-Coates. Lt-Col, Coldstream; CO of 2nd Battalion June 1944. *Died* 9 May 1982. **P.35, 44, 52, 62, 78, 79, 91**

Cobbold, Robert: Major R.N., Welsh Guards, *Killed* 27 May 1944. **P.58**

Coke, Richard: Captain, Scots Guards, MC, DSO. Later developed forestry in Norfolk; High Sheriff 1981. Once killed 50 brace of grouse with one gun. Obituary *Daily Telegraph* 21 May 2001. **P.79**

Colvin, Dick: Brigadier, Grenadier Guards, DSO, CO 22nd Guards Brigade Nov 1942-Jan 1945; succ. by Brig H.R.Norman. **P.19**

Conlin, Clive: Lieutenant, K.R.R.C; Ampleforth O42. **P.68**

Constantine & Bone, Bishop of: *vere* Constantine-Hippone. Bishop Emile-Jean-Francois Thiénard, consecrated 1924, died 1945. A predecessor at Hippo was the great St Augustine. **P.33**

Cooper, Michael: Lieutenant, Grenadier Guards. Not otherwise identified. **P.60**

Cop, Brigadier: abbr. for Copland-Griffiths

Copland-Griffiths, F.A.V.: Lt-Colonel, DSO. CO 1st Brigade to 1943, then on Staff at Washington. In 1942 he had been Military Force Commander for a plan to reoccupy Alderney (Channel Islands). *Died* 1962. **P.18, 20**

Corbould, Bill: Captain F.W.P, Coldstream Guards, MD (Brother of Peter, cousin of Fr Edward Corbould, Ampleforth E51). **P.55**

Corbould, Peter: Brother of Bill; two sons at Ampleforth B58, B64. **P.28**

Cowan, Sir Walter: Admiral, RN, OC Commandos, Africa & Italy, esp. at R.Garigliano. DSO & Bar. Commissioned 1890, commanded a battleship at Jutland 1916, Rear-Admiral 1918; retired 1931, volunteered 1940 aged 68; captured by Italians 1942, exchanged 1943. *Died* 1956. **P.36**

Cowper, John: Ampleforth A33. **P.16**

Cramer, John: Lieutenant, Royal Engineers, 272 Field Company Royal Engineers, attached 46 Div.; Ampleforth O39. Later R&D, Metal Box Company. *Died* 23 May 2004. [Editor's brother] **P.19, 45**

Crouch, Ray: Coldstream Guards; not yet traced. **P.60**

Crowder, Peter: Lieutenant, later Major, Coldstream Guards, ADC to General Leese (GOC Eighth Army after Montgomery), Barrister, QC, MP (Hillingdon-Ruislip-Northwood), active in Parliament. *Died* 1999. P.39, 66

Cubitt, Victor: Lieutenant, Grenadier Gds, *Killed* 27 June 1944. Ampleforth C40. (219030) . **P.18, 57, 60, 63**

Cumming, Hugh: *No data yet,* **P.32**

Cuthbert, David: *No data yet.* **P.49**

Dalrymple, John: Viscount, Lt-Colonel, Scots Guards, CO 1st Bn 1942-43, CO Scots Guards 1949-52, retd 1953; 13th Earl of Stair 1961, KCVO 1978. *Died* 1996.. **P.19**

Darling, Colonel Douglas Lyall: Lt-Colonel, Rifle Brigade, DSO & Bar, MC & Bar. *Died* 1978. **P.83**

Davies-Scourfield, Colonel David: Major, Welsh Guards, MC. He took command in Feb 1944 with a badly poisoned foot, but won the MC within a month. *Died* 1998 aged 87. **P.44, 62**

Denny, Tony: Major A.M., Grenadier Guards, MD. **P.43**

Dietz, Fr Frederick: from 1937 Procurator-General of the Catholic Foreign Mission Society of America (Maryknoll Fathers). **P.84, 90**

Dixon, Danny: Lt-Colonel D.S.T.B., KBE, active in Belfast Parliament, farming and racing –'Never seen in Northern Ireland during Ascot week'. (*See also* www.newulsterbiography.co.uk) **P.94**

Dommersen, Fr Sidney: from Archdiocese of Westminster. Later Parish Priest at Richmond upon Thames, where he commissioned a modern church, now listed Grade II. **P.19, 65**

Dowd, Fr Hugh: Chaplain, later Principal Chaplain (1952), from Diocese of Hexham & Newcastle. MBE. *Died* 1953. **P.96**

Dowling, Fr: one of 21 Jesuits from Irish Province. 11th General Hospital 1943; 167 Field Ambulance, then with Royal Artillery, Central Mediterranean Force; 4th Bn, Oxford & Bucks, 1944; 21st Army Group: Germany 1945-46. **P.16**

Egan, Jim: Not yet identified. **P.19, 67**

Egerton, John: Major, R.E.M.E. **P.45**

Faber, Tom: Lieutenant, Grenadier Guards, MD. Ampleforth C40. Later prominent in Hampshire in land, farm management and the family brewing business. **P.43, 60**

Falkiner, Terence: Major Sir Terence Bt., Coldstream Guards, CO 3rd Battalion at Salerno. **P.23**

Faller, Ben: Lieutenant, Coldstream Guards . *Killed* 12 August 1944. **P.41*, 44**

Fane, Julian: Younger son of 14th Earl of Westmoreland. Saw action in 1943 but invalided out. Later well-known as a writer. *Died* December 2009. **P.32**

Farnell-Watson, Arthur: Lieutenant, Coldstream Guards, MD. *Died* 2006. **P.39**

Farran, Roy: Army in Egypt, Crete Italy; wounded, POW, escaped. Active as SAS leader; Palestine. MC & 2 Bars, DSO. Settled in Canada 1951 (farming, politics).*Died* 2006. Obituary *Daily Telegraph* 5 June 2006. Wrote *Winged Dagger*, London, 1954, & other books. **P.99**

Farrer, Guardsman: Not yet identified. **P.44**

Field, Toffee: C.O., 1st Field Ambulance (ch.35). **P.83**

Firth, Raymond: Not yet identified. **P.84**

Fitzalan Howard: here usually Howard, *whom see.*

Fitzroy, Humphrey: Captain F.H.M., Coldstream Guards. **P.81**

Forster, Stewart: Brigadier, Coldstream Guards, CO 1st Guards Brigade 1943; retired (stroke) 1944. *Died* 1965. **P.20, 33**

Fortescue, Desmond: (J.D.G.), Captain, Coldstream Guards. Latwr High Sheriff of Cornwall 1966. **P.74**

Fraser, Hugh: Major H.C.P.J., Lovat Scouts, MBE. Ampleforth C35. Later MP, Cabinet Minister. *Died* 1984. **P.33**

Fraser, Ian: Lieutenant, Scots Guards, MC. Ampleforth O41. Cousin of Lovat Frasers; Chairman, Rolls-Royce Motors 1971. *Died* 2003. **P.63, 81**

Fraser, Sandy: Captain A.H., Lovat Scouts, MD. Ampleforth C37. **P.71**

Furze, Ronnie: Not yet identified. **P.56**

Gaffney, Fr William: Diocese of Northampton, Chaplain. Parish Priest, Marlow 1959-75. *Died* 1985. **P.18**

Gale, Peter: Lieutenant, Coldstream Guards. *Killed* 21 June 1944. **P.63**

Gavin, Paddy: Fr George's driver. Not otherwise identified. **P.69**

Gawlina, Bishop: Bishop of Polish Military Vicariate 1933-47. *Died* 1964. **P.49**

George VI, King: The King (1936-52) visited Italian front July 1944. **P.9, 67*, 69**

Gibson-Watt, James David: Major, Welsh Guards, MC & Bar. Later MP for Hereford, Forestry Commissioner. *Died* 2002. Obituary, *Daily Telegraph* 13 Feb 2002. **P.40, 44**

Gilbey, Ralph: Lieutenant, R.N., 15/19 King's Royal Hussars; Ampleforth O42. Later Director, Shire Horse Society. Retired. **P.94**

Gordon, Queenie: *No data yet.* **P.106**

Goschen, John: Lt-Colonel, Grenadier Guards; later 3rd Viscount Goschen of Hawkhurst, KCBE, Conservative politician. **P.54**

Goulburn, Eddie: Lt-Colonel E.H., Grenadier Guards, DSO. Later CO 2nd Armoured Grenadier Bn at Arnhem 1944.CO Grenadier Guards 1948-50. (28083). **P.91**

Grant, Rev.: Church of Scotland chaplain. **P.46**

Green, Henry: Major, H.J.L.,Coldstream Guards, DSO MD. Later CO 2 Bn Coldstream 1955, Federal Infantry Bde, Malaya 1959. Racing commentator, BBC 1948-54. *Died* 1986. **P.37, 41, 67**

Gregson-Ellis, Philip: Brigadier, Grenadier Guards, CB. GOC 5 Division 1944; later Commandant, Staff College, Camberley. *Died* 1956. **P.33, 35**

Grey-Turner, Elston: Colonel, Regimental Medical Officer, 2 Bn Coldstream Guards 1942-45. Later Vice-President, B.M.A. 1976-79. (cf. his diary, Welcome Library GC/96, http: //library.wellcome.ac.uk). *Died* 1984. **P. 18, 21, 23, 41*, 42, 44*, 46, 54, 58, 61, 62, 65, 79*, 83, 96**

Gurney, Jocelyn: Lt- Colonel, Welsh Guards, CO 3rd Battalion 1945. DSO. *Died* 1973. P.54, 62

Guthrie, Arthur: Anglican Chaplain, Grenadier Guards (218714).. **P.54**

Harford, Charles: Captain, Coldstream Guards, MD. **P.17**

Harkness, Jack: Captain, Grenadier Guards, MC, MD. **P.60**

Harris, Bill: Captain, Coldstream Guards. *Unconfirmed.* **P.21, 28, 78**

Hawkesworth, General: Maj-General J.L.I., (East Yorks Regiment), GOC 46 Division 1943-44. *Died* 3 June 1945, aged 52 (heart attack). 'Ginger'. **P.44**

Haydon, Charles: Brigadier, Middlesex Regiment, DSO. **P.12, 35, 40, 67**

Hayley, Tim: Lieutenant, Welsh Guards. *Killed* 27 May 1944, **P.58**

Heber-Percy,Algy: Lt-Colonel, Grenadier Guards, DSO, later Brigadier. *Died* 1961. **P.18, 45**

Hill, Roddy: Colonel, CO, 5th Bn, Coldstream Guards (Italy, Normandy, Belgium, Germany), DSO; first Lord Lieutenant of Gwent 1974. *Died* 1998 aged 94.**P.23**

Hilton-Green, Michael: Lieutenant F.M., Coldstream Guards, *Killed* 9 February 1944 (Monte Ornito), **P.39**

Hodgkinson, Col. Reggie: Major, 2 Welsh Guards, MC, NW Europe 1944-5. **P.91**

Hodgson, Edward: Lt-Colonel D.E.P., Welsh Guards, OBE. **P.18, 35**

Hogarth, Sandy: Grenadiers 1922, contemporary of Fr George; visited Rome with Gds Band, & died there Sept 1944. **P.70**

Hollings, Michael: Lieutenant, Coldstream Guards, MC Tunis; later Fr Michael Hollings, Archdiocese of Westminster, Chaplain at Oxford University 1959-70, Parish Priest Southall & Bayswater. *Died* 1997. Obituary, *Independent* 22 Feb 1997. **P.41, 59, 64**

Holman, Fr Nicholas OSB: Monk of Downside 1929, Chaplain, with BEF 1940, at Dieppe, later with 26 Armoured Bde at Gothic Line, & Cyprus 1956. Administrator, then Abbot, of Fort Augustus 1968-91. *Died* 4 August 2001. Obituary, *Daily Telegraph* 12 Aug 2001. **P.67, 90**

Horlick: Perhaps Lt-Colonel Sir James Horlick, 4th Baronet. Lt-Colonel, Coldstream Guards, MC 1917, MBE. *Died* 1972. Nephew of inventor of malted milk products. **P.90**

Howard, Martin: Captain, Grenadier; *vere* Fitzalan Howard, Lord Martin O1941, Italy, wounded Normandy, Palestine. DL, Sheriff of North Yorkshire. Restored Carlton Towers. Obituary *Daily Telegraph* 11 Aug 2003. **P.94**

Howard, Michael: Major-General, 3 Bn Scots Guards, *vere* Fitzalan Howard, Lord Michael, GCVO, CB, CBE, MC;. Ampleforth B35. Cambridge, Italy, NW Europe, Palestine, Malaya, Suez, Germany. Retd. 1971. Colonel of the Life Guards, Marshal of the Diplomatic Corps. *Died* 2007 aged 91. Obituary *Daily Telegraph* 5 Nov 2007. **P.64, 81, 91, 95**

Howard, Miles: Lt-Colonel, Grenadier Guards; *vere* Fitzalan Howard, Miles, Ampleforth O34, Oxford. KG, GCVO, CB, MC, later 17th Duke of Norfolk.

Service BEF 1940, Italy, Germany, Kenya, Ministry of Defence; City Banker, Earl Marshal. *Died* 2002. Obituary *Guardian* 26 Jun 2001. **P.8, 29, 64**

Howard-Stepney, Taffy (Stafford): (from August 1950 Howard) Lieutenant, later Captain, S.V.S.Howard, Coldstream Guards (121335). Married daughter of Sir James Horlick above. Liberal Candidate for Parliament 1949. **P.55, 56**

Howland-Jackson, Geoffrey: Captain A.G., Grenadier Guards, MBE. **P.43**

Huntington, Charles: Captain A.C., Grenadier Guards, MD. **P.35**

Hyde, Bobby: *No data yet.* **P.20**

Inskip, John: Scots Guards ? *No data yet.* **P.79***

Jackson, Tom: Lieutenant, Coldstream Guards. *Killed* 10 February 1944. **P.39,41**

Jameson, Stan: *No data yet.* **P.54**

Jones-Davis: non-Catholic Chaplain to Welsh Guards. **P.63**

Keightley, General Charles: 5/6 Dragoons, a year above Fr George at Sandhurst. In N.Africa & Italy, Commander of 6 Armoured Div., then 78 Infantry Div., ending the War GOC Eighth Army V Corps. Later C-in-C for troops in both Korea and Suez operations. **P.19**

Kendrew, Brigadier 'Joe': Lt-Colonel D.A., Leicestershire Regiment, DSO . Later in command of 29 Infantry Bde at Battle of the Hook, 28 May 1953 (Korea).. **P.43**

Kevill, Tony: Major A.J., R.A., MD; Ampleforth O38, *Died* 2006. **P.94**

Knox, Bryce: Major B.M., R.A., MC. **P.80***

Lamb, Fr Francis: Chaplain, a Carmelite from Jerusalem. *Died* 1950 (?) **P.94**

Lambert, John Henry: Captain, Grenadier Guards. **P.55**

Lascelles, George: Viscount, Lieutenant, Grenadier Guards. Eldest grandchild of George V; later Earl of Harewood. Italy: wounded, taken prisoner 18 June 1944. In Colditz: sentenced to death by Hitler. Later famous as director of English National Opera, other music, & development of Harewood House. Obituary *Daily Telegraph* 11 Jul 2011. **P.62**

Lumley, John: Lieutenant, Coldstream Guards. *Killed* 6 December 1944. **P.63, 79**

Lumley-Savile, Henry: Lieutenant, Grenadier Guards (262099). **P.62**

Macdonald, Andrew: Major, Lovat Scouts. Ampleforth 1926. Scottish landowner (sheep, forestry); donated site for Commando Memorial, Spean Bridge. *Died* 1995. **P.71**

Macdonald, Johnny: Major J.L. Macdonld of Tote, Lovat Scouts 1938, Phantoms 1942: Faroes, Africa, Italy, NW Europe. Ampleforth W38. Developed farming in Skye & electronics in Chelsea. *Died* 2002. **P.33**

Maclean, Peter: Captain, Grenadier Guards. *Killed* 20 February 1944. **P.43**

Macmillan, Harold: Captain, Grenadier Guards, wounded Somme 1916. From 1943, Minister Resident at Allied Forces Headquarters, later Prime Minister. *Died* 1986 Obituary, *Guardian* 30 December 1986. **P.100**

Magrath, John: Captain, Intelligence Corps. El Alamein, Italy. Captured Urbino (solo) 28 Aug 1944 ahead of 4th Indian Div. (celebration there in 1994). Later worked for Shell, took First (Fr. & It.) London, taught till retirement. Ampleforth B39. *Died* 2005. Obituary *Independent* Nov 2005. [Editor's brother-in law] **P.46, 59**

Makins, Colonel Willie: Lt-Colonel Sir William, 3rd Baronet, Welsh Guards. Sudan, BEF, N.Africa, Italy, Commandant Sandhurst, 1944. Retd 1948. **P.35**

Matheson, Colonel: CO 7th Bn Argyll & Sutherland Highlanders. **P.29**

Maude, Christopher: Captain, Welsh Guards. *Killed* 27 May 1944 (Cassino; 149154). **P.58**

Mayes, Andrew: officer prisoner found in hospital at/near Villach, Austria. *No data yet.* **P.88**

McCabe, Fr Leonard: Passionist, Chaplain. Later Broadway, Middleton Lodge, Highgate. *Died* 2 April 1966. **P.36**

McCreery, General R.L.: Commission 12th Royal Lancers. MC 1918, DSO 1940. BEF, GOC X Corps,Fifth Army at Salerno, GOC Eighth Army (Gothic Line to Austria).KBE 1945, GCB, retd 1949. *Died* 1967. **P.12, 44**

McCreton, Fr Basil: Diocese of Middlesbrough, Senior Chaplain, Middle East. Commission 1931 (49633), MC 1940. Retd (health) 1948, returned to Diocese. *Died* 15 May 1970. **P.93**

McHugh, Fr Brendan: monk of Prinknash, Chaplain. Commission 1941 RAF (101837). First local Prior of Pluscarden (later Abbey) 1948-51. Prinknash 1951. *Died* 29 April 1958. **P.46**

Melfa: In this battle on the Melfa river, the Canadian Westminster Regiment's Major John Mahony won the VC. **P.58***

Michael and Reggie: i.e. Fitzalan-Howard. *See* Howard above & Secondé below

Mikaelovitch, *vere* **Mihailovic, Draza:** leader in Yugoslavia of the Chetniks, or pro-Serbain and royalist opponents of the later successful Communist partisans under Josip Broz (Tito). **P.98, 99**

Montagu, Eustace: *No data yet.* **P.56**

Montagu-Douglas-Scott, Andrew: Brigadier, Irish Guards. DSO (Tunisia) & Bar (Anzio), MD. *Died* 1971. P.67

Monty: General Bernard Montgomery, GOC Eighth Army from Alamein to Italy, Later GOC 21st Army Group, NW Europe. Later knighted, Field Marshal, Viscount. **P.10, 30***

Morris, Dai: Captain Owen David, 3rd Bn Welsh Guards (2734526), MC 1944. **P.45, 75, 83, 87**

Muir, Robin: Lieutenant, 2nd Bn Coldstream. Hospital, jaundice March 1944.**P.62**

Murdoch, Bob: 2nd Lt C.R. 1942 (240632). **P.60**

Murray, H: Major-General, Cameron Highlanders (Sandhurst contemporary of Fr George), commander of 6th (Guards) Armoured Division from 21 August 1944 (coming straight from 51st Highland Div. in Normandy). **P.70, 76**

Needham, Pat: Major J.R.P., Grenadier Guards. Later (1961) 5th Earl of Kilmorey. *Died* 1977. **P.48, 54**

Neilson, Andrew: Captain A.S., 2 Bn Scots Guards, DSO. (219064) *Killed* 16 July 1944. **P.49, 52, 60, 66**

Nelson, John: Lt-Colonel, Grenadier Guards MC; later knighted, retired as Commandant, British Sector, Berlin 1966-68. *Died* 1993. **P.62, 66, 75***

Nicolson, Nigel: Captain, Grenadier Guards, son of Harold. Later Conservative MP, & partner in publisher Weidenfeld & Nicolson. **P.82**

Noel, David: D.F.D. Lieutenant (later Lt-Colonel) 1st Bn Coldstream Guards BEF 1940, N.Africa, Malaya (MD) Later Defence Attaché, Kabul 1965-67. Ampleforth C33. *Died* 1974. **P.55**

Norman, Hugh: Colonel/Brigadier H.R., Coldstream Guards. CO 2nd Battalion, Africa & Italy (wounded). Signed citation for Fr George's MC. High Sheriff of Kent 1957. *Died* 1979. **P.12, 34, 44, 62, 91, 96**

O'Rourke, Sgt: MM, wounded (River Arno 1944). **P.70**

Ord, Fr Edward, 'Natty': Diocese of Hexham & Newcastle, Chaplain.1939+ TD 1970. *Died* c.1985. **P.44**

Paget-Cooke, Dicky: Commission 1940 (117907), later Captain R.A., Grenadier Guards MBE. **P.18, 55**

Palmer, Bob: *No data yet.* **P.41*, 44, 74, 75**

Penn, John: Lieutenant, 3 Bn Grenadier Guards, MC 1944. **P.48**

Perrott, Peter: Fr George wrote 'Killed' under 5 or 6 August 1944; more likely 7 August, but he is not listed by War Graves Commission. **P.68**

Phantoms: A secret regiment, officially known as GHQ Reconnaissance Regiment, whose purpose was to gather information on the exact position of forward troops during fluid battlefield conditions, thus reducing the likelihood of 'friendly fire'. Phantom's officers had a unique reporting structure which by-passed all intermediary ranks and fed information - including intelligence on what Britain's allies were up to - directly to the most senior generals. They often earned the envy of senior regular soldiers, whose information they sometimes had to contradict. (*Daily Telegraph,* article 21.12.2002) **P.32, 33**

Pickford, Corporal: Grenadier Guards, Stretcher bearer; *No data yet.* **P.41**

Pike, Bill: (Brigade HQ, Irish Guards, Tunisia); *No data yet.* **P.18**

Ponsonby, Ashley: Captain A.C.G., Coldstream Guards, MC. **P.78**

Pope Pius XII: Was Nuncio (Ambassador) in Munich, Bavaria (by special agreement instead of Berlin) before Nazis, then Secretary of State to Pius XI. Elected Pope 1939. *Died* 1958. **P.9, 69**

Poston, Colonel: R.A.M.C.(?) Lt. Col. R I Poston, 125 Field Amb. 1940. **P.13, 57**

Prescott, John: Lt-Colonel J.L, R.A.S.C., MD. **P.35**

Price, Colonel 'Proggins': 102 Field Regiment, R.A. **P.18**

Rea, Abbot: Dom Gregorio Diamare was Abbot of Monte Cassino 1909 till his death 6 September 1945: his successor was Dom Ildefonso Rea 1945-1971 (retd). **P.55**

Reyntiens, Michael: Lieutenant R.A.M., Scots Guards; Ampleforth E42 *Died* 2003. **P.34**

Robin, Raoul: *No data yet.* **P.68**

Rochford, Tony: Lieutenant A.W.T., Irish Guards. Ampleforth B38, *Killed* 30 March 1943, Tunisia. **P.19**

Roome, Oliver: R.E., later Maj-General, *Died* 2009. **P.75**

Roosevelt, President: President of the USA, elected 1932, 1936, 1940, 1944: played very large part in the defeat of the Axis powers 1939-45. *Died* suddenly 12 April 1945. **P.35, 100**

Rowley, Joshua: Captain, Grenadier Guards (POW). Later Chairman, Suffolk County Council 1974, Deputy Secretary National Trust 1952, *Died* 1997. Obituary *Independent* 27 Feb 1997. **P.56**

Rudd, Brian: Lieutenant B.R., Coldstream Guards (288230); *Killed* 7 August 1944. **P.68**

Rudesind, Fr: *see* Brookes

Sangster, Sandy: Colonel J.H., R.A.M.C., MD. **P.45, 64**

Scott, Andrew: Brigadier C.A.M.D., Irish Guards, DSO. **P.47,76**

Secondé, Reggie: Major R.L., Coldstream Guards, North Africa, Italy. MD. Retd 1949; later Ambassador Chile, Romania, Venezuela KCMG CVO. **P.41, 81, 84**

Scrope, 'Bunty': Brigadier A.C., Green Howards, OBE; Ampleforth 1925. **P.86**

Sharp E.M.: Lieutenant, Scots Guards. *Killed* 8 May 1944. **P.56**

Sheridan, Roddy: Lieutenant R.G., Coldstream Guards (176757). Wounded 17 Feb 1944. Diplomatic Service 1946-77. **P.41**

Skimming, Ian: Major I.E.B.,2nd Bn Coldstream Guards, MD. CO, 2 Coy Feb 1944. Chairman, Bowring Group 1972. **P.41**

Southey, Bob: ? R.A.M.C. *No data yet.* **P.54, 86**

Sparks, Guardsman: *Killed* 15 October (IGF) 1944. Not listed by War Graves Commission]. **P.75**

Spencer, Hugh: Lieutenant, Coldstream Guards. *Killed* .28 May 1944. **P.60**

Steele, Billy: Either Lt William Steele 359382 or Lt William Steele 216451; both were doctors. **P.74**

Stepney: *see* Taffy Howard-Stepney

Stern, Eric: *No data yet.* **P.43**

Stewart-Brown, Bunty: Colonel W.S., Coldstream Guards, DSO, MD. **P.18,21,34**

Streatfeild-Moore (sic), Tom: Lieutenant T.E., Grenadier Guards. *Killed* 5 August 1944. **P.75**

Tebourba Boys: 2nd Battalion, the Hampshire Regiment (later Royal), part of 1st (Guards) Brigade in 78 Div when it nearly reached Tunis in November 1942, Two Guards Battalions in the Brigade were held in Algeria from want of transport. The Hampshires alone held the nearby town of Tebourba for 4 days (29 Nov+) against overwhelming enemy numbers despite losing nearly 500 casualties. The 3rd Bn Welsh Guards took their place in the Brigade. **P.18**

Thorogood, Guardsman: D.G.J., Coldstream Guards, MD. **P.40**

Tito, Josip Broz: leader of Communist partisans in Yugoslavia, later Marshal and a Communist leader successfully independent of Moscow. **P. 88*, 90, 98-100**

Toler, David: Major, Coldstream Guards, MC. **P.56**

Tomaschek, Fr: Austrian Catholic chaplain for the German 90th Light Division, Salzburg Diocese, captured in Tunisia, May 1944. **P.26***

Trafford, Eddie: *No data yet.* **P.49, 56**

Tweedie, Pat: Lt-Colonel P.C.C., Cameron Highlanders Ampleforth C29. **P.29**

Twining, Dick: Captain R.C., Welsh Guards. *Killed* 9 April 1943. **P.19**

Twomey, Larry: Lt-Colonel, R.A., DSO; Ampleforth 1922. **P.55, 76**

Utley, Jim: In Italy as tutor to an Italian family in the 1920's. He remained here for the rest of his life, except for a short break during the 1939-45 war; c.1950-70 served in British Legation to the Holy See. **P.69**

Verney, General: Maj-General G.L., Grenadier Guards, DSO. GOC 7th Armoured Division NW Europe August 1944, GOC 1st Gds Brigade, Italy, March 1945; later Military Commandant in Vienna. **P.84, 91**

Vinci, Contessa da: Leading member of a still prominent family, including the artist & polymath Leonardo. **P.84**

Von Arnim: German Commander in both wars; had commands in Poland and France 1939-40, then wounded in Russia. GOC Afrika Korps in last phase of

African campaign: surrendered to 4th Indian Division at the fall of Tunis 12 May 1943. **P.26**

Von Loehr: General Alexander von L., former Commander of 12th Army in the Balkans; Commander-in-Chief South-East. Tried & sentenced to death (Belgrade 1947) as responsible for mass murders of Yugoslav civil inhabitants. **P.88***

Von Vietinghoff: General Heinrich-Gottfried, C-in-C Army Group C, Italy **P.88**

Walker, Drill Sergeant: *No data yet.* **P.57**

Walkcr, Guardsman: *No data yet.* **P.58**

Walzer, Abbot Raphael: monk of Beuron, SW Germany 1907; 4th Abbot (aged 29) 1918-1937; in exile (France & Algeria) from opposition to Nazis; (re)founded Weingarten, Neresheim & others, clothed over 130 monks: community in 1935 numbered almost 300. Friend of Edith Stein. Chaplain to French Army in Algeria, founded theology school at Rivet for German POWs 1943. *Died* 1966. **P.16**

Ward, Fr Edward: Diocese of Leeds, Chaplain. **P.13**

Watkins, Gordon: Inns of Court Regiment, Intelligence Officer attached Derbyshire Yeomanry, then Guards Brigade Press Officer. Ampleforth B37. 2nd DY was the 1st Regiment to enter Tunis. For this *see* http://www.paoyeomanry.co.uk/DYC/Persons/DYCWW2.htm. **P.20, 49**

Way, Tony: Major A.G., Grenadier Guards, MC,MD. **P.60***

Whitwell, Stephen: Lieutenant, Coldstream Guards, MC. **P.41, 44, 52**

Williams, Elladwr: Lieutenant, Welsh Guards. **P.45**

Williams, Ewart: Grenadier Battalion. **P.35**

Windsor-Clive, Bob: Lieutenant, Coldstream Guards; later Brigadier, died 14 October 2003. **P.20, 56, 62, 71**

Young, CSM: Scots Guards, S Coy. **P.79**

ABBREVIATIONS, ACRONYMS, TERMS
Used in the text

A.A.: Anti-Aircraft (artillery, gunners)

A.D.S.: Advanced Dressing Station

A.F.H.Q.: Allied Forces Headquarters

A.P.: Armour-piercing; sometimes Anti-Personnel

A/T: Anti-Tank

A.G.R.A.: Army Group Royal Artillery.

A.Y.: Ayrshire Yeomanry

Basutos: Men from what is now Lesotho, in southern Africa

B.E.M.: British Empire Medal (Military Division)

Bee-hive: A 5lb (2.2kg) explosive charge to blast holes in house walls in street fighting. It was shaped like an old straw beehive, with the wide end against the wall, to direct the force.

Bn: Battalion

B.N.A.F.: British North African Forces

Bomb-happy: Shaken; or disorientated for a time, or shock.

Bound: A defined area, usually marked in some way

Bren: The Bren Gun was the standard British machine gun during the whole War, originally a Czech design. 'Bren' is from Brno & Enfield, two arms factories in the 1930's.

Brewing up: Cooking over a fire; but also commonly of a hit tank bursting into flames.

Cameronian: Queen's Own Cameron Highlanders

Chetniks: Those who had fought for Mihailović (Mikaelovitch) against Tito

C. in C.: Commander in Chief

C.of S.: Church of Scotland

CGT/C.G.T.: Compagnie Générale Transatlantique, known as the French Line

C.M.: Congregation of the Mission (alias Vincentians, Lazarists)

C.O.: Commanding Officer

Col: Colonel

Compo: Compo rations, the Army's standard food pack.

C.P.: Congregation of the Passion, Passionists: an order of preachers

C.P.R.: Canadian Pacific Railway; some of their ferries were requisitioned for war service.

Croix de Guerre: French military decoration

C.Q.M.: Company Quartermaster

C.S.M.: Company Sergeant-Major

D.A.Q.M.G.: Deputy Assistant Quartermaster-General

D.C.M.: Distinguished Conduct Medal (replaced by C.G.C., Conspicuous Gallantry Cross 1993)

D.F.: Defensive Fire, but controlled, not reactive.

Dingo: Two-man armoured car, nicknamed from an Australian wild dog.

D.P.s: Displaced persons (civilian refugees)

D.S.O.: Distinguished Service Order

Easter Duty: Minimum Obligation for Catholics; annual Sacraments of Confession & Communion, between Ash Wednesday & Pentecost

Echelons: Battalion transport, F, A, B (for Fighting, Supply, Backup)

F.D.S.: Forward Dressing Station

Fantails: Amphibious armoured troop carriers

Focke-Wulf: Maker (and so type) of German aircraft

Gdsn: Guardsman (title or rank of ordinary soldier in the Guards regiments)

G.I.: US servicemen. Originally 'Galvanised Iron' (for army use), then' Government Issue', then 'General Infantry'.

G.O.C.: General Officer in Command

Greek corporal: a portable altar stone and cloth with relics sewn into it.

Greenjackets: Original form of the Rifle Brigade 1800, who wore green not red, operating as sharpshooters.

Hards: Slipway or inclined launching surface for boats, or at ferries

H.C.: Abbreviation for Holy Communion

H.E.: High explosive

I.O.: Intelligent Officer (at any level)

I.R.T.D.: Infantry Reinforcement Transit Depot.

KOYLI: Kings Own Yorkshire Light Infantry.

Kraut: Troops' name for German troops ('vegetable', 'cabbage')

L.C.I.: Landing Craft, Infantry

L.C.T.: Landing Craft, Tank

Leonine prayers: Prayers at the end of Mass for the defence of the Holy See's temporal sovereignty, instituted by Pope Leo XIII (1884); later changed to the conversion of Russia (1929-65).

L.O.C.K.: League of Christ the King (a Catholic youth organisation)

Luftwaffe: German Air Force 1933-45

Manloads: How much a man can carry in portering: could be quite large.

M.C.: Military Cross

M.D.: Mentioned in Dispatches (in Notes on People Named)

M.D.S. : Mobile Dressing Station

Medloc route: Mediterranean Line of Communication: 4 trains per 24 hours, Milan-Calais or Marseille-Dieppe through the second half of 1945, for leave or return. (http: //www.movcon.org.uk/History/Snippets/MEDLOC.htm)

M.E.F.: Middle East Forces

Mick(s): Irish Guards

M.M.: Military Medal

M.O.: Medical Officer

M.T.: Motor Transport

M.T.O. : Motor Transport Officer

Nebelwerfer: German battlefield rocket launcher, for smoke, explosive or (in design) chemicals or gas.

N.C.O.s: Non-commissioned Officers – Sergeant Majors, Sargeants etc.

Ohio: SS Ohio was a tanker regarded as saviour of Malta in August 1942, when it reached the island when most supply ships were being sunk.

O.P.: Observation Post

O.T.C.: Officers' Training Corps (now Combined Cadet Force)

Overs: Artillery rounds which fall beyond the target: frequent in hill country.

Panniers: Motor-cycle side containers.

Phantoms: See List of People

Porcian height: T.Macaulay, in *'The Battle of Lake Regillus'* (Lays of Ancient Rome), thought L.Caterno was the place of this legendary battle in defence of ancient Rome. Perhaps it was.

P.O.W. : Prisoner of War

Provost: Military Police

Q.M.: Quarter Master (supply)

R.A.M.C.: Royal Army Medical Corps

R.A.P.: Regimental Aid Post

R.A.S.C: Royal Army Service Corps

R.B.: Rifle Brigade (regiment)

Reveille: 'Revalley', the call to get up, originally a bugle call.

R.S.M.: Regimental Sergeant-Major

R.T.O.: Railway Transport Officer

Sangar: Foxhole on the surface made with rocks when digging was impossible.

Sappers: Field engineers (R.E.)

S.C.F.: Senior Chaplain to the Forces (in any theatre)

Schu-mine: Nasty if you trod on it.

Shermans: American design of tank (M4) much used 1942 onwards by British as well as American forces. Though faster, and much more numerous (50,000 were built) it was not as well gunned or armoured as the German Panther and Tiger tanks. According to Imperial War Museum, Manchester, about the same number of Russian T34 tanks were produced, but over a much longer period.

Sitrep: Situation Report

Spandaus: German standard machine gun

Spark out: Fall into deep sleep

Stern Gang: Anti-British terrorist group in Palestine 1940-48

Stonk: Concentrated artillery fire, perhaps from 'standard concentrated fire'

Stuka: German dive-bomber

T.A.B.: Inoculation against typhoid & paratyphoid

Tac. H.Q.: Tactical Headquarters

Taylorcraft: Light aircraft for observation, British & U.S. http: //www.taylorcraft.org.uk/

T.C.V. : Troop carrying vehicle (ie a lorry filled with rows of seats)

T.G.W.U.: Transport & General Workers' Union, later merged with Amicus to form Unite (2007)

Underfeature: Subordinate summit of a mountain.

V.1 or V1: German pilotless bomb (from 1944, 'Doodlebug')

V.E. Day: 8 May 1945: the celebration of the end of the war in Europe (VJ Day was 15 August)

Vere: In fact, or other editorial correction of date, name etc.

Whitlow: Viral finger or thumb infection: can be serious.

Yalta agreement: Churchill, Roosevelt, and Stalin with their staffs met at Yalta in the Crimea in February 1945 to agree on the post-war world and the disposition of various national claims.

The job was well done, however, and the Armoured Brigade passed through the gap and took Kairouan. The infantry following up got dive-bombed several times by Stukas on the open roads in the plain and suffered some casualties. We were now in touch with the advancing 8th Army who had taken Sousse, but the enemy whom we hoped to trap had slipped away to the north. The 8th Army had enough troops to follow him up, so after a day's march northwards along an open road subject to frequent dive-bombing attacks, we were withdrawn, by the way we had come to the forest of Kesra. Just as we got back to our area at 5 a.m. the Coldstream had one of their many unlucky accidents with a T.C.V., which turned over, killing one of the men inside and injuring others.

Brigadier Cop left us at Kesra on

Fr George's handwritten original (1947-48).   Ampleforth BX26; 18 x 23 cm

SOURCES & REFERENCES

Local

Obituary of Fr George Forbes, *Ampleforth Journal*, 96: 2 (1991) p33; Available online

Ampleforth & the War: privately published list of old boys who served during the War 1939-45

Benedictine chaplains: more on individuals online at www.plantata.org.uk.

Military

Commonwealth War Graves Commission, at www.cwgc.org

Ulstermen, www.newulsterbiography.co.uk

London Gazette: commissions, promotions, awards (& so identity or date), www.london-gazette.co.uk. Not easy to use.

Forces Reunited: all ranks (but gaps, duplications, multiple surnames), www.forcesreunited.org.uk

Forces War Records (similar limitations), www.forces-war-records.co.uk

Murphy's Register, www.militaryarchive.co.uk/murphys-register.html

Army Lists, the Public Record Office, Regimental archives, for those in a position to reach them.

General

New Oxford Dictionary of Biography (online for subscribers or libraries www.oxforddnb.com)

Who's Who, and *Who Was Who*, various editions/volumes

Obituaries from *Daily Telegraph, Guardian, Independent, Times*: often online for the last ten years or so.

Google (www.google.com, www.google.co.uk, &c), which often points to –

Wikipedia, the universal stand-by (fewer distractions and side-issues)

LIST OF IMAGES

Fr George's own images unless noted below

* *Photo*: Fr Alban Crossley OSB

† *Photo*: Capt. J.P. Magrath

LIST OF MAPS

Chaplains worked on a brigade or battalion level, or smaller. Only large-scale maps would help to follow the details of Fr George's account. Even the excellent Italian Touring Club 1: 200,000 maps do not include most of the names he gives (there are 440 in all), many of them perhaps only hamlets or even farmsteads. In a book of this size we can only therefore give outline maps to show the essentials of the campaign, which in our time is probably no longer very familiar to people. We have included only the key places: to do anything else would have made the maps illegible. And on this scale it is difficult to be exact. The arrows give a general impression of the movement of the armies, but there is not space to do justice to the German dispositions in defence.

Fr George the railwayman: off to Camp by a well-planned train
(Gilling East 1956). He was said to know the timetable by heart.

INDEX

For references to persons, see p.101